C000089895

Collins Foundation World Atlas

Collins
An imprint of HarperCollinsPublishers
77-85 Fulham Palace Road
LondonW6 8JB

© HarperCollinsPublishers 2005
Maps © Collins Bartholomew Ltd 2005

First published 2005, reprinted 2007
ISBN-13 978-0-00-719547-3 School edition
ISBN-10 0-00-719547-8 School edition
ISBN-13 978-0-00-719546-6 Trade edition
ISBN-10 0-00-719546-X Trade edition

Imp 002

Collins ® is a registered trademark of
HarperCollinsPublishers Ltd

The contents of this edition of the Collins
Foundation World Atlas are believed correct at the
time of printing. Nevertheless the publishers can
accept no responsibility for errors or omissions,
changes in the detail given, or for any expense or
loss thereby caused.

Printed and bound in Thailand

British Library Cataloguing in Publication Data
A catalogue record for this book is available from
the British Library.

All mapping in this atlas is generated from Collins
Bartholomew digital databases. Collins
Bartholomew, the UK's leading independent
geographical information supplier, can provide a
digital, custom, and premium mapping service to a
variety of markets. For further information:
Tel: +44 (0) 141 306 3752
e-mail: collinsbartholomew@harpercollins.co.uk

Visit our website at: www.collinsbartholomew.com

www.collinseducation.com/atlases

A Political Map

Map A uses different colours to show clearly the shape of each country. A line is used to represent the international boundary around each country. It is possible to see the relative areas of the countries. Capital cities and other major cities are shown by symbols on a Political map.

B Rainfall Map

The colours on Map B represent areas which have the same range of annual rainfall. From this type of map it is possible to find the wettest or driest region in a country. Rainfall maps are often accompanied by climate graphs such as the one shown at the bottom of the opposite page.

Using Atlas Maps

An atlas includes different kinds of maps and diagrams. The different parts of an atlas page are shown on the map below which is a reduced version of page 22 in the atlas. In order to understand maps it is important to understand the labels and information which appear on each page. The example below is a reference map which

Using Atlas Maps

1 Page Title
The page title explains what area or topic the map covers.

2 Page Number
The page number is essential when using the index or contents page.

3 Letters and Numbers
These form a grid which make it easy to find places listed in the index eg Naples is in grid square F4.

4 Lines of Latitude
These show how far north or south of the Equator a place is located.

5 Facts Box
Information in the Facts Box is subdivided into various categories. An icon (or symbol) identifies each of the categories which are explained below.

Facts Box...

The information listed in the **Facts about...** box is explained below.

Landscape: Indicates the area and highest point.

Population: Lists the total population and the average number of people living in one square kilometre.

Settlement: Shows the percentage of the population living in cities and towns. The main towns and cities are also listed.

Land Use: Main crops grown and the main industries in the region are identified here.

Development Indicators: Four indicators are shown here.

Life expectancy: The number of years a newborn child can expect to survive.

GNP per capita: The annual value of production of goods and services of a country, per person.

Primary school enrolment: The total of all ages enrolled at primary level as a percentage of primary age children.

Access to safe water: Percentage of the population with reasonable access to sufficient safe water.

Lines of Latitude and Longitude 4

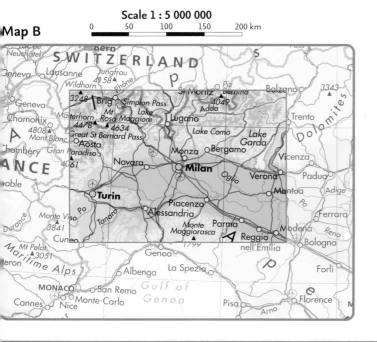

South Pole

North Pole

60°W
30°W
Greenwich Meridian
30°E
60°E
90°E

South Pole

3 Lines of Longitude

Measuring Distance

The scale of a map can also be used to work out how far it is between two places. In the example below, the straight line distance between Brasília and Salvador on the map of Brazil is 7 cm. The scale of the map is 1 : 15 000 000. Therefore 7 cm on the map represents 7 X 15 000 000 cm or 105 000 000 cm on the ground. Converted to kilometres this is 1050 km. The real distance between Brasília and Salvador is therefore 1050 km on the ground.

Scale 1 : 15 000 000

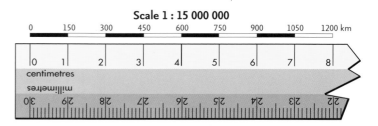

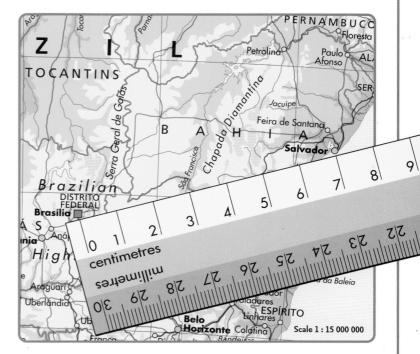

Map B

Scale 1 : 5 000 000

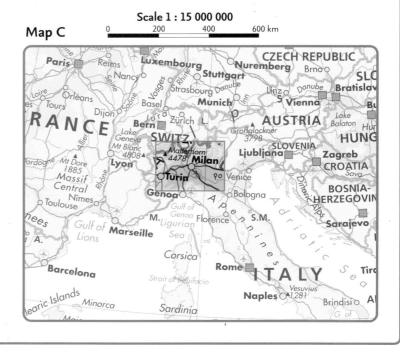

Map C

Scale 1 : 15 000 000

Symbols

Maps use **symbols** to show the location of a feature and to give information about that feature. The symbols used on each map in this atlas are explained in the **key** to each map.

Symbols used on maps can be dots, diagrams, lines or area colours. They vary in colour, size and shape. The numbered captions to the map below help explain some of the symbols used on the maps in this atlas.

Different styles of type are also used to show differences between features, for example, country names are shown in large bold capitals, small water features, rivers and lakes in small italics.

Using Grids

The map on the left shows the British Isles. Lines of latitude and longitude are numbered in 2° intervals in the map frame. These form a **grid** on the map. Large letters and numbers, together known as **alphanumerics,** are used to label the horizontal and vertical columns made by the grid.

The alphanumerics can be used to identify the **grid square** in which a feature is located, for example

> Ben Nevis is in D5,
> Snowdon in D3,
> The Wash in G3.

1 ⁓ **River**
The largest and most important rivers are shown.

2 ✈ **Airport**
Main international airports are shown.

3 ◉ **Large City**
This symbol is used to show cities with over 500 000 people.

4 ■ **Capital City**
All capital cities, large or small are shown with the same symbol.

5 ⟋ **Railway**
Road
Railways and roads are the main links between the towns and cities.

6 ☁ **Lake**
Lakes and areas of water are shown in a pale blue tint.

7 ○ **Other Town or City**
Cities or towns with less than 500 000 people are shown as a small yellow dot.

8 ⟍ **International Boundary**
International boundaries mark the edges between one country and another. They give a country a distinctive shape by which we can often identify it.

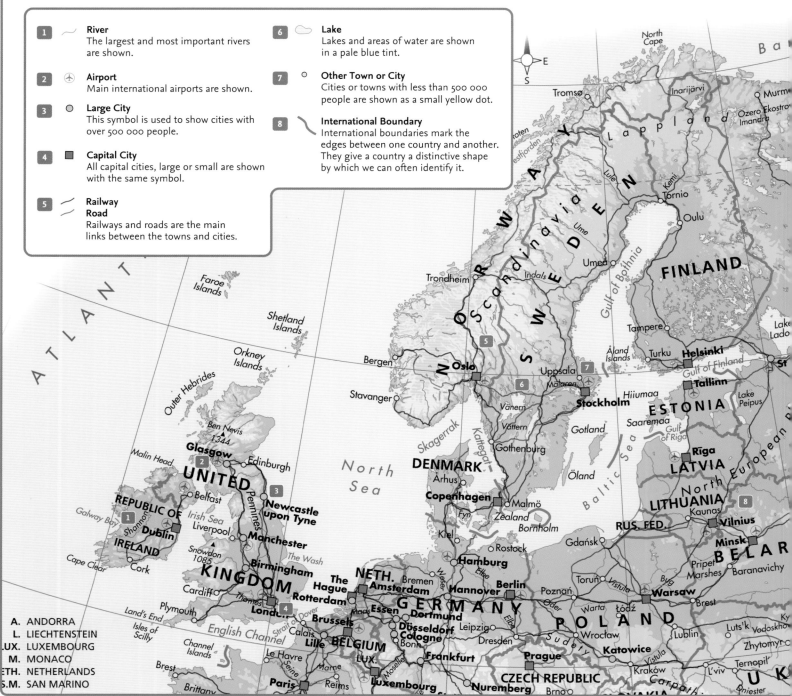

A. ANDORRA
L. LIECHTENSTEIN
LUX. LUXEMBOURG
M. MONACO
ETH. NETHERLANDS
S.M. SAN MARINO

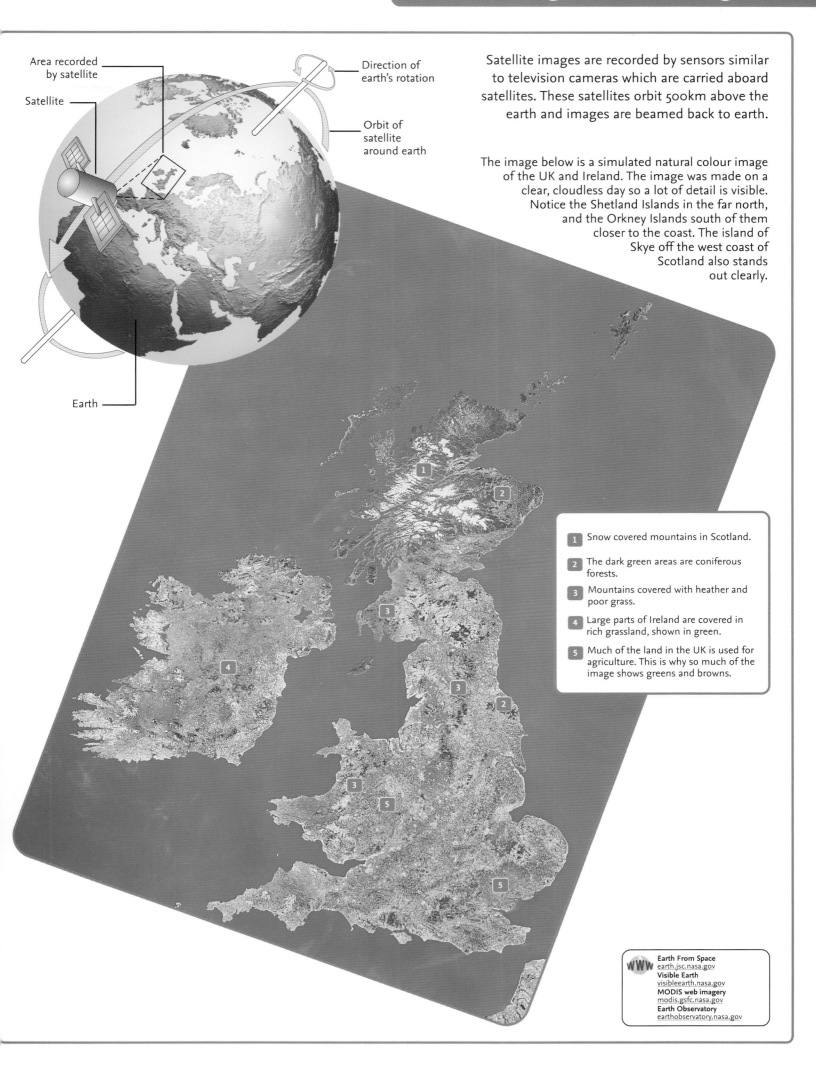

Area recorded by satellite

Satellite

Earth

Direction of earth's rotation

Orbit of satellite around earth

Satellite images are recorded by sensors similar to television cameras which are carried aboard satellites. These satellites orbit 500km above the earth and images are beamed back to earth.

The image below is a simulated natural colour image of the UK and Ireland. The image was made on a clear, cloudless day so a lot of detail is visible. Notice the Shetland Islands in the far north, and the Orkney Islands south of them closer to the coast. The island of Skye off the west coast of Scotland also stands out clearly.

1 Snow covered mountains in Scotland.

2 The dark green areas are coniferous forests.

3 Mountains covered with heather and poor grass.

4 Large parts of Ireland are covered in rich grassland, shown in green.

5 Much of the land in the UK is used for agriculture. This is why so much of the image shows greens and browns.

WWW **Earth From Space**
earth.jsc.nasa.gov
Visible Earth
visibleearth.nasa.gov
MODIS web imagery
modis.gsfc.nasa.gov
Earth Observatory
earthobservatory.nasa.gov

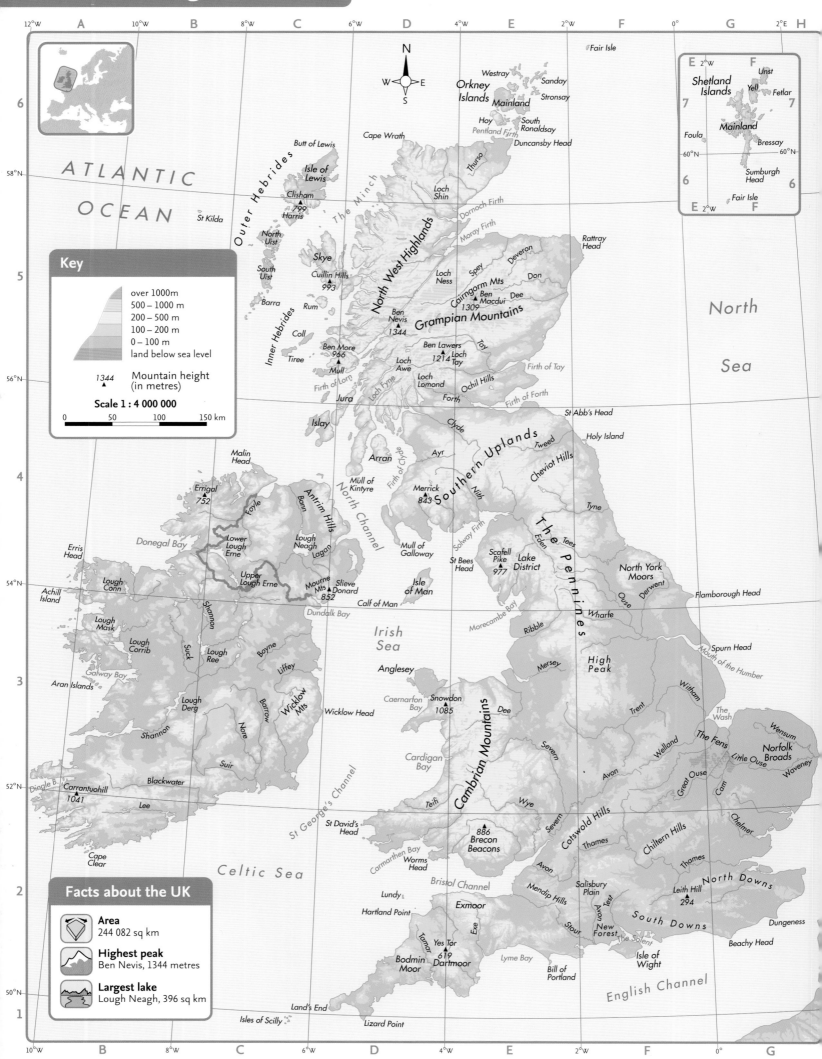

Key

over 1000m
500 – 1000 m
200 – 500 m
100 – 200 m
0 – 100 m
land below sea level

▲ 1344   Mountain height (in metres)

Scale 1 : 4 000 000

0   50   100   150 km

Facts about the UK

Area
244 082 sq km

Highest peak
Ben Nevis, 1344 metres

Largest lake
Lough Neagh, 396 sq km

ATLANTIC OCEAN

North Sea

Irish Sea

Celtic Sea

English Channel

St George's Channel

Bristol Channel

North Channel

The Minch

Shetland Islands
Mainland
Foula
Unst
Yell
Fetlar
Bressay
Sumburgh Head
Fair Isle

Fair Isle
Orkney Islands
Westray
Sanday
Stronsay
Mainland
Hoy
South Ronaldsay
Duncansby Head
Pentland Firth
Cape Wrath
Thurso

Butt of Lewis
Isle of Lewis
Outer Hebrides
Clisham ▲ 799
Harris
North Uist
St Kilda
South Uist
Barra

Skye
Cuillin Hills ▲ 993
Rum
Coll
Tiree
Inner Hebrides

North West Highlands
Loch Shin
Dornoch Firth
Moray Firth
Loch Ness
Spey
Deveron
Rattray Head
Cairngorm Mts
Ben Macdui ▲ 1309
Dee
Don
Ben Nevis ▲ 1344
Grampian Mountains
Ben More ▲ 966
Mull
Firth of Lorn
Loch Awe
Ben Lawers ▲ 1214
Loch Tay
Tay
Firth of Tay
Jura
Islay
Loch Fyne
Loch Lomond
Ochil Hills
Forth
Firth of Forth
St Abb's Head

Arran
Firth of Clyde
Clyde
Ayr
Nith
Southern Uplands
Tweed
Cheviot Hills
Holy Island
Merrick ▲ 843
Mull of Kintyre
Mull of Galloway
St Bees Head
Solway Firth
Tyne

Malin Head
Errigal ▲ 752
Foyle
Antrim Hills
Bann
North Channel
Donegal Bay
Lower Lough Erne
Lough Neagh
Lagan
Upper Lough Erne
Mourne Mts ▲ 852
Slieve Donard
Dundalk Bay
Calf of Man
Isle of Man

Erris Head
Achill Island
Lough Conn
Lough Mask
Lough Corrib
Galway Bay
Aran Islands
Shannon
Suck
Lough Ree
Boyne
Lough Derg
Shannon
Barrow
Nore
Suir
Liffey
Wicklow Mts
Wicklow Head

Scafell Pike ▲ 977
Lake District
Eden
Tees
The Pennines
North York Moors
Derwent
Flamborough Head
Morecambe Bay
Wharfe
Ouse
Ribble
Spurn Head
Mouth of the Humber
Mersey
High Peak
Witham
The Wash

Carrantuohill ▲ 1041
Dingle B.
Lee
Blackwater
Cape Clear

Anglesey
Caernarfon Bay
Snowdon ▲ 1085
Cardigan Bay
Dee
Cambrian Mountains
Teifi
St David's Head
Severn
Trent
Avon
Great Ouse
Welland
The Fens
Cam
Little Ouse
Norfolk Broads
Wensum
Woveney

886 ▲ Brecon Beacons
Carmarthen Bay
Worms Head
Wye
Severn
Cotswold Hills
Thames
Chiltern Hills
Thames
Chelmer
Leith Hill ▲ 294
North Downs
Dungeness

Lundy
Hartland Point
Exmoor
Exe
Mendip Hills
Avon
Salisbury Plain
Avon
Test
South Downs
Beachy Head

Bodmin Moor
Yes Tor ▲ 619
Dartmoor
Tamar
Lyme Bay
Bill of Portland
New Forest
The Solent
Isle of Wight

Land's End
Isles of Scilly
Lizard Point

Lambert Azimuthal Equal Area projection

Key

▬▬	Country boundary
──	Internal boundary
──	Road
──	Railway
⋯⋯	Ferry route
✈	Airport
■	Capital city
●	Large town or city
○	Other town or city

Scale 1 : 4 000 000

0   50   100   150 km

WWW National Statistics Online
www.statistics.gov.uk
Department for Transport
www.dft.gov.uk
UK at a glance
www.statistics.gov.uk/glance

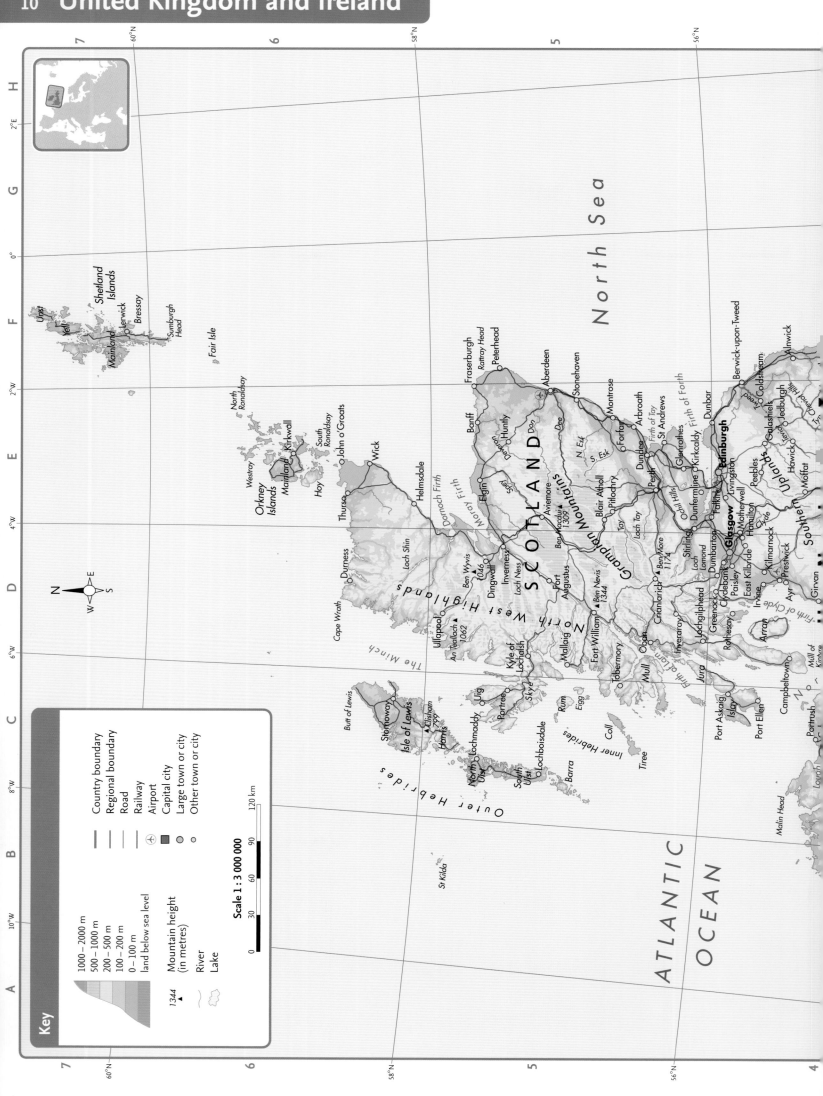

Key

	1000 – 2000 m
	500 – 1000 m
	200 – 500 m
	100 – 200 m
	0 – 100 m
	land below sea level

	Country boundary
	Regional boundary
	Road
	Railway
✈	Airport
■	Capital city
●	Large town or city
○	Other town or city

1344 ▲ Mountain height (in metres)

⌇ River

⌇ Lake

Scale 1 : 3 000 000

0   30   60   90   120 km

N
W — E
S

ATLANTIC

OCEAN

North Sea

SCOTLAND

North West Highlands

Grampian Mountains

Southern Uplands

Shetland Islands

Unst
Yell
Mainland
Lerwick
Bressay
Sumburgh Head

Fair Isle

Orkney Islands
Westray
North Ronaldsay
Mainland
Kirkwall
Hoy
South Ronaldsay
John o'Groats

Cape Wrath
Durness
Thurso
Wick
Helmsdale

Butt of Lewis
Stornoway
Isle of Lewis
Clisham 799 ▲
Harris
Lochmaddy
North Uist
Uig
Portree
Skye
Lochboisdale
South Uist
Barra

St Kilda

Outer Hebrides

The Minch

Loch Shin
Ben Wyvis 1046 ▲
Dingwall
Inverness
Loch Ness
Fort Augustus

An Teallach 1062 ▲
Ullapool

Dornoch Firth
Moray Firth
Elgin
Spey
Aviemore
Ben Macdui 1309 ▲
Blair Atholl
Pitlochry

Banff
Huntly
Deveron
Don
Dee
N. Esk
S. Esk

Fraserburgh
Rattray Head
Peterhead
Aberdeen
Stonehaven
Montrose
Arbroath
Forfar
Firth of Tay
St Andrews

Kyle of Lochalsh
Mallaig
Rum
Eigg
Fort William
Ben Nevis 1344 ▲
Tobermory
Mull
Coll
Tiree
Inner Hebrides

Oban
Crianlarich
Ben More 1174 ▲
Loch Lomond
Loch
Inveraray
Lochgilphead
Firth of Lorn

Port Askaig
Islay
Port Ellen
Jura
Campbeltown
Mull of Kintyre

Arran
Rothesay
Greenock
Clydebank
Dumbarton
Paisley
Glasgow
East Kilbride
Kilmarnock
Irvine
Prestwick
Ayr
Girvan
Firth of Clyde

Stirling
Falkirk
Livingston
Motherwell
Hamilton
Clyde

Dunfermline
Kirkcaldy
Perth
Tay
Loch Tay
Ochil Hills
Glenrothes
Firth of Forth

Edinburgh
Peebles
Galashiels
Hawick
Moffat
Jedburgh
Tweed
Lammermuir Hills
Cheviot Hills
Dunbar
Berwick-upon-Tweed
Coldstream
Alnwick

Malin Head
Portrush

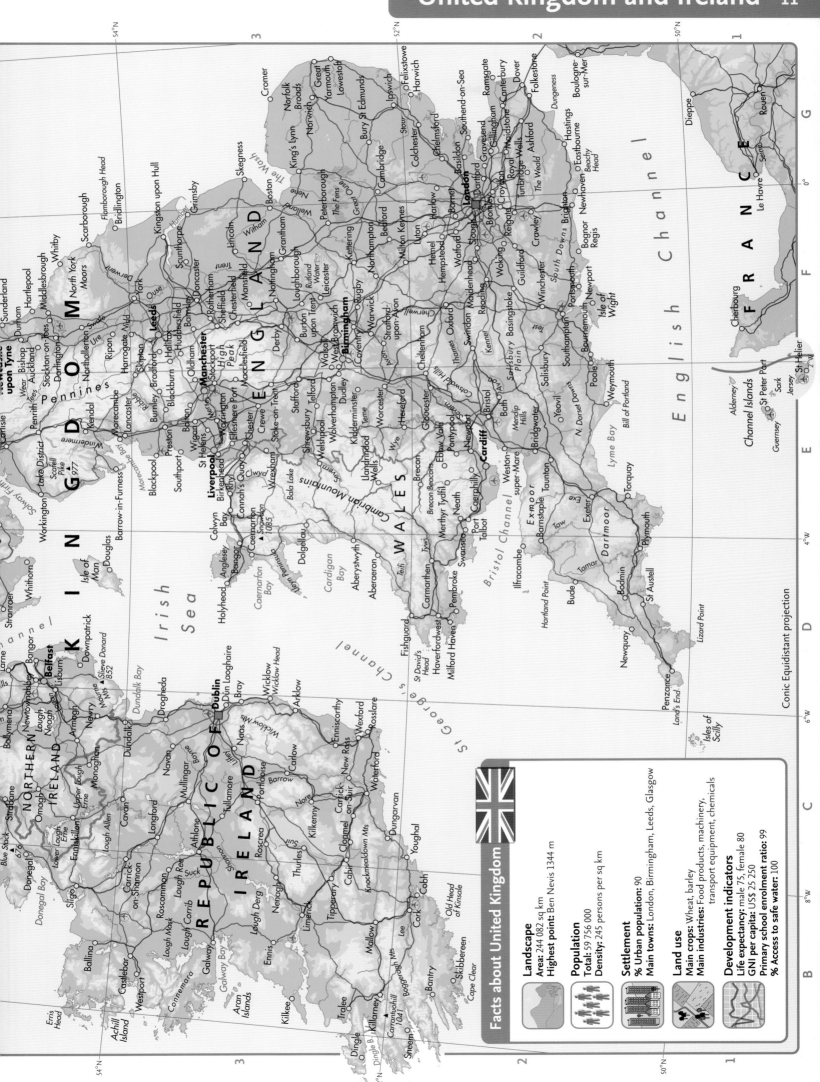

Facts about United Kingdom

Landscape
Area: 244 082 sq km
Highest point: Ben Nevis 1344 m

Population
Total: 59 756 000
Density: 245 persons per sq km

Settlement
% Urban population: 90
Main towns: London, Birmingham, Leeds, Glasgow

Land use
Main crops: Wheat, barley
Main industries: Food products, machinery, transport equipment, chemicals

Development indicators
Life expectancy: male 75, female 80
GNI per capita: US$ 25 250
Primary school enrolment ratio: 99
% Access to safe water: 100

Conic Equidistant projection

United Kingdom

SCOTLAND
Edinburgh

NORTHERN
IRELAND Belfast

SCOTLAND

REPUBLIC
OF
IRELAND

WALES ENGLAND

Cardiff

London

SCOTLAND
1. INVERCLYDE
2. WEST DUNBARTONSHIRE
3. EAST RENFREWSHIRE
4. GLASGOW CITY
5. EAST DUNBARTONSHIRE
6. NORTH LANARKSHIRE
7. FALKIRK
8. CLACKMANNANSHIRE
9. WEST LOTHIAN
10. EDINBURGH

SHETLAND
Lerwick

ORKNEY
Kirkwall

WESTERN
ISLES
Stornoway

HIGHLAND
Inverness

MORAY
Elgin

ABERDEEN-
SHIRE
ABERDEEN
Aberdeen

SCOTLAND

PERTH &
KINROSS
Perth

ANGUS
Forfar
DUNDEE
Dundee

FIFE
Glenrothes

ARGYLL
AND BUTE
Lochgilphead

STIRLING
Stirling
Alloa
8
Falkirk 7

EAST
LOTHIAN
Haddington
Edinburgh
10
Dalkeith
MIDLOTHIAN

SCOTTISH
Newtown
St Boswells
BORDERS

Dumbarton 2
Paisley 1
RENFREWSHIRE
3

Kirkintilloch
5
Glasgow
4

9
Livingston

Motherwell
6
Hamilton
SOUTH
LANARKSHIRE

NORTH
AYRSHIRE
Irvine
North

Kilmarnock
EAST
AYRSHIRE

SOUTH
AYRSHIRE
Ayr

DUMFRIES
Dumfries

NORTHUMBERLAND
Morpeth

Newcastle upon Tyne

Ballycastle
MOYLE
COLERAINE Ballymoney
Coleraine Ballymoney
Limavady LIMAVADY
Londonderry
DERRY

NORTHERN IRELAND
1. NEWTOWNABBEY
2. CARRICKFERGUS
3. BELFAST
4. CASTLEREAGH
5. NORTH DOWN

N
W E
S

ENGLAND
1. MIDDLESBROUGH
2. READING
3. WOKINGHAM
4. BRACKNELL FOREST
5. WINDSOR & MAIDENHEAD
6. SLOUGH
7. THURROCK
8. MEDWAY

WALES
1. BLAENAU GWENT
2. MERTHYR TYDFIL
3. TORFAEN
4. CAERPHILLY

Boroughs of Greater London

Barking and Dagenham	Hammersmith and Fulham	Merton
Barnet	Haringey	Newham
Bexley	Harrow	Redbridge
Brent	Havering	Richmond upon Thames
Bromley	Hillingdon	Southwark
Camden	Hounslow	Sutton
City of London	Islington	Tower Hamlets
Croydon	Kensington and Chelsea	Waltham Forest
Ealing	Kingston upon Thames	Wandsworth
Enfield	(admin. centre for Surrey)	Westminster
Greenwich	Lambeth	
Hackney	Lewisham	

FRANCE

BELGIUM

REPUBLIC OF IRELAND

NORTHERN IRELAND

ENGLAND
WALES

CUMBRIA
NORTH YORKSHIRE
EAST RIDING OF YORKSHIRE
LANCASHIRE
WEST YORKSHIRE
SOUTH YORKSHIRE
DERBYSHIRE
GREATER MANCHESTER
MERSEYSIDE
CHESHIRE
NORTH LINCOLNSHIRE
NORTH EAST LINCOLNSHIRE
LINCOLNSHIRE
NOTTINGHAMSHIRE
STAFFORDSHIRE
SHROPSHIRE
WEST MIDLANDS
WARWICKSHIRE
WORCESTERSHIRE
HEREFORDSHIRE
LEICESTERSHIRE
RUTLAND
NORTHAMPTONSHIRE
NORFOLK
SUFFOLK
CAMBRIDGESHIRE
BEDFORDSHIRE
ESSEX
HERTFORDSHIRE
BUCKINGHAMSHIRE
OXFORDSHIRE
GLOUCESTERSHIRE
GREATER LONDON
KENT
SURREY
WEST SUSSEX
EAST SUSSEX
HAMPSHIRE
WILTSHIRE
SOMERSET
DORSET
DEVON
CORNWALL
BRIGHTON & HOVE
BOURNEMOUTH
POOLE
TORBAY
PLYMOUTH

POWYS
GWYNEDD
CONWY
DENBIGHSHIRE
FLINTSHIRE
CEREDIGION
CARMARTHENSHIRE
PEMBROKESHIRE
MONMOUTHSHIRE
GLAMORGAN

ISLE OF MAN
ISLE OF ANGLESEY
ISLES OF SCILLY
CHANNEL ISLANDS (UK)
ALDERNEY
GUERNSEY
JERSEY

Conic Equidistant projection

National Statistics Online
www.statistics.gov.uk
The Scottish Parliament
www.scottish.parliament.uk
Northern Ireland Office
www.nio.gov.uk
The National Assembly for Wales
www.wales.gov.uk

Annual rainfall

There is little variation between winter and summer. The highest rainfall is in the west where winds from the sea blow against the mountains and hills. Central and eastern areas are more sheltered and have lower rainfall.

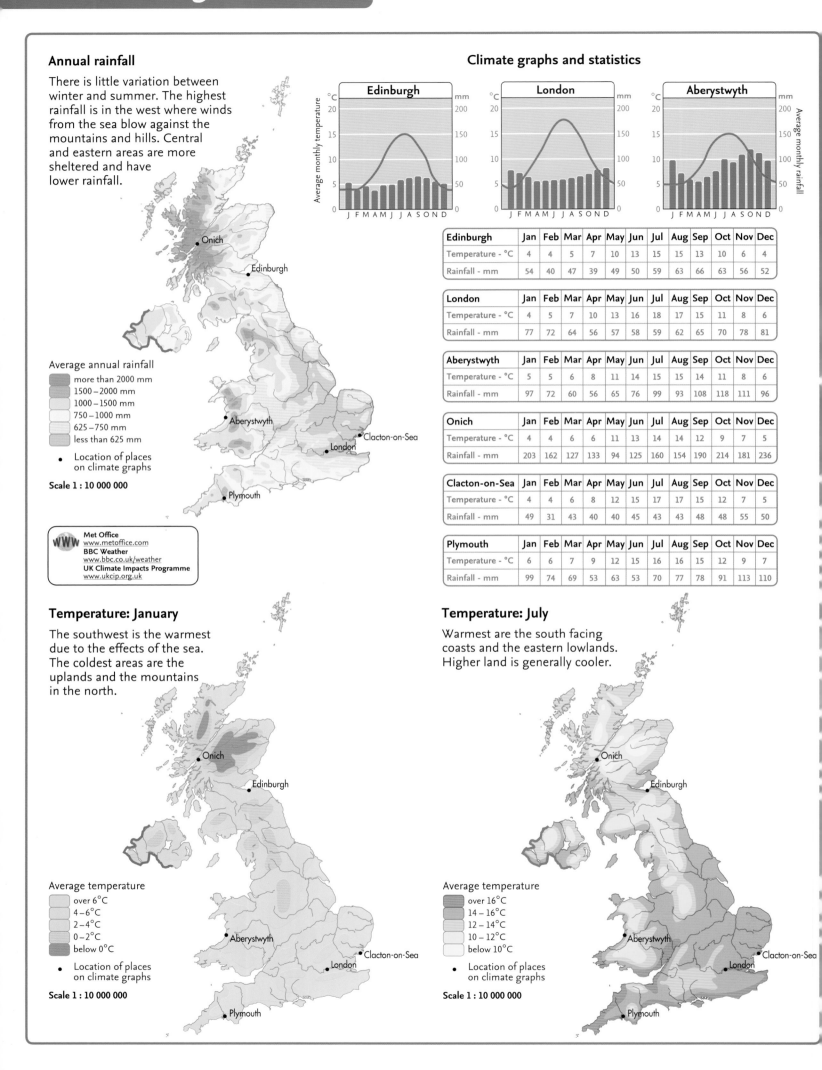

Average annual rainfall
- more than 2000 mm
- 1500 – 2000 mm
- 1000 – 1500 mm
- 750 – 1000 mm
- 625 – 750 mm
- less than 625 mm
- • Location of places on climate graphs

Scale 1 : 10 000 000

WWW
Met Office
www.metoffice.com
BBC Weather
www.bbc.co.uk/weather
UK Climate Impacts Programme
www.ukcip.org.uk

Climate graphs and statistics

Edinburgh
°C / mm

London
°C / mm

Aberystwyth
°C / mm

Edinburgh	Jan	Feb	Mar	Apr	May	Jun	Jul	Aug	Sep	Oct	Nov	Dec
Temperature - °C	4	4	5	7	10	13	15	15	13	10	6	4
Rainfall - mm	54	40	47	39	49	50	59	63	66	63	56	52

London	Jan	Feb	Mar	Apr	May	Jun	Jul	Aug	Sep	Oct	Nov	Dec
Temperature - °C	4	5	7	10	13	16	18	17	15	11	8	6
Rainfall - mm	77	72	64	56	57	58	59	62	65	70	78	81

Aberystwyth	Jan	Feb	Mar	Apr	May	Jun	Jul	Aug	Sep	Oct	Nov	Dec
Temperature - °C	5	5	6	8	11	14	15	15	14	11	8	6
Rainfall - mm	97	72	60	56	65	76	99	93	108	118	111	96

Onich	Jan	Feb	Mar	Apr	May	Jun	Jul	Aug	Sep	Oct	Nov	Dec
Temperature - °C	4	4	6	6	11	13	14	14	12	9	7	5
Rainfall - mm	203	162	127	133	94	125	160	154	190	214	181	236

Clacton-on-Sea	Jan	Feb	Mar	Apr	May	Jun	Jul	Aug	Sep	Oct	Nov	Dec
Temperature - °C	4	4	6	8	12	15	17	17	15	12	7	5
Rainfall - mm	49	31	43	40	40	45	43	43	48	48	55	50

Plymouth	Jan	Feb	Mar	Apr	May	Jun	Jul	Aug	Sep	Oct	Nov	Dec
Temperature - °C	6	6	7	9	12	15	16	16	15	12	9	7
Rainfall - mm	99	74	69	53	63	53	70	77	78	91	113	110

Temperature: January

The southwest is the warmest due to the effects of the sea. The coldest areas are the uplands and the mountains in the north.

Average temperature
- over 6°C
- 4 – 6°C
- 2 – 4°C
- 0 – 2°C
- below 0°C
- • Location of places on climate graphs

Scale 1 : 10 000 000

Temperature: July

Warmest are the south facing coasts and the eastern lowlands. Higher land is generally cooler.

Average temperature
- over 16°C
- 14 – 16°C
- 12 – 14°C
- 10 – 12°C
- below 10°C
- • Location of places on climate graphs

Scale 1 : 10 000 000

Population density

The greatest concentration of population in the United Kingdom is found in the areas immediately surrounding London where the number of persons per square kilometre is more than 500 times greater than in the Scottish Highlands. The total population of England is greater than the sum of the populations of Scotland, Wales and Northern Ireland.

Persons per sq km
- over 150
- 10 – 150
- 0 – 10

Cities and towns
- over 5 000 000
- 1 000 000 – 5 000 000
- 500 000 – 1 000 000
- 100 000 – 500 000
- 20 000 – 100 000

Scale 1 : 5 000 000

Population by country
2000

- England
- Scotland
- Wales
- N Ireland

2.8%
4.9%
8.6%
83.7%

UK total 59 756 000

Increase in population
1901-2041

Dotted line indicates projected population

Population in millions

1901 1911 1921 1931 1951 1961 1971 1981 2001 2021 2041

— United Kingdom
— England
— Scotland
— Wales
— N Ireland

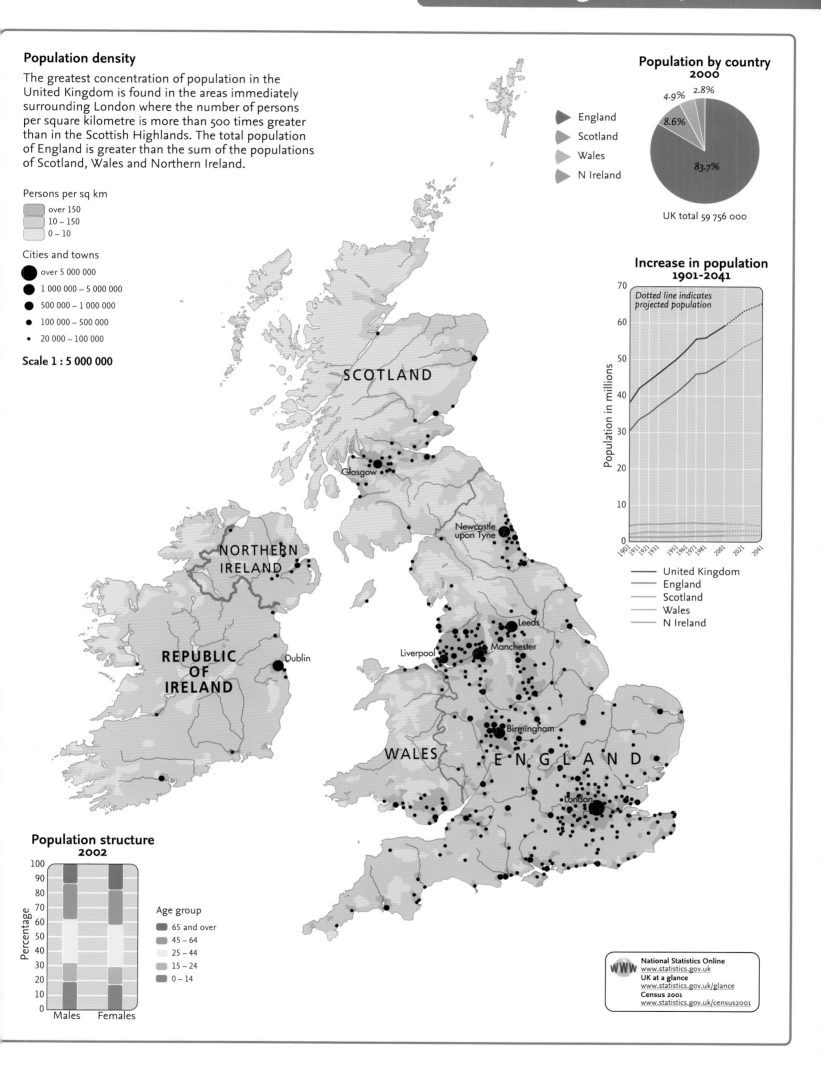

SCOTLAND

Glasgow

NORTHERN IRELAND

REPUBLIC OF IRELAND

Dublin

Newcastle upon Tyne

Leeds

Liverpool   Manchester

Birmingham

WALES   E N G L A N D

London

Population structure
2002

Percentage

100 90 80 70 60 50 40 30 20 10 0

Males   Females

Age group
- 65 and over
- 45 – 64
- 25 – 44
- 15 – 24
- 0 – 14

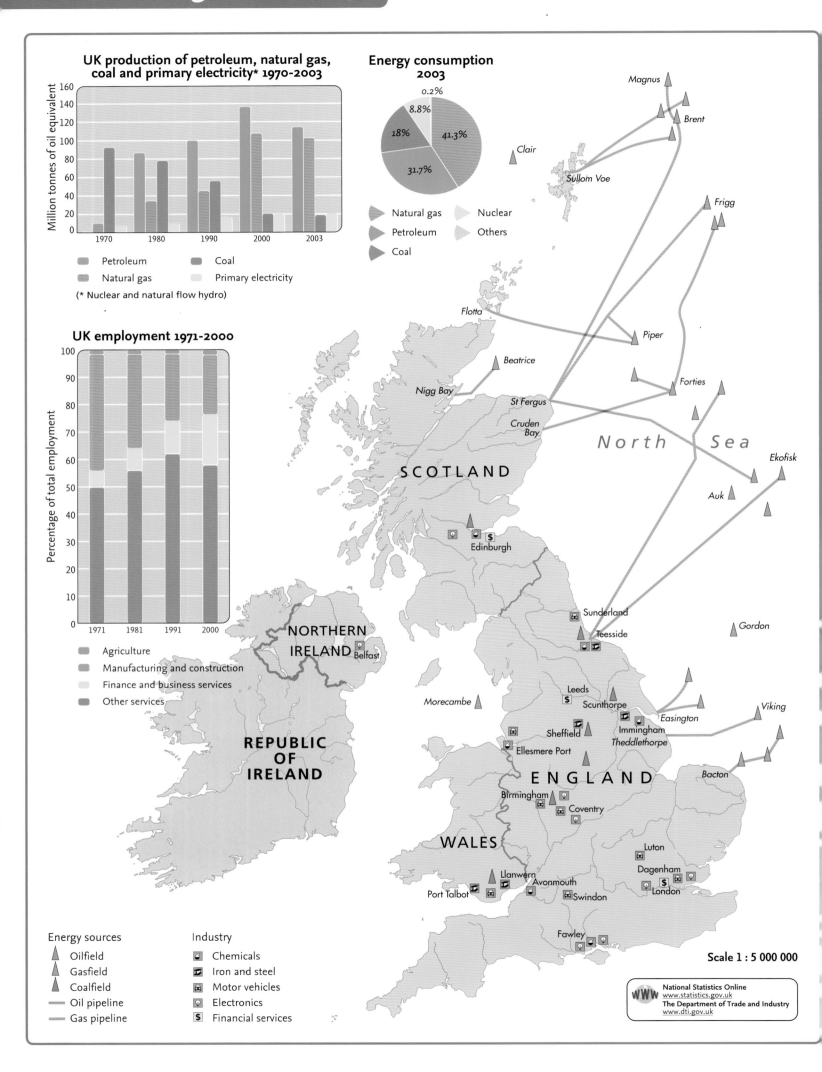

UK production of petroleum, natural gas, coal and primary electricity* 1970-2003

Million tonnes of oil equivalent

160
140
120
100
80
60
40
20

1970   1980   1990   2000   2003

- Petroleum
- Natural gas
- Coal
- Primary electricity

(* Nuclear and natural flow hydro)

Energy consumption 2003

0.2%
8.8%
18%
41.3%
31.7%

- Natural gas
- Petroleum
- Coal
- Nuclear
- Others

UK employment 1971-2000

Percentage of total employment

100
90
80
70
60
50
40
30
20
10
0

1971   1981   1991   2000

- Agriculture
- Manufacturing and construction
- Finance and business services
- Other services

Magnus
Brent
Clair
Sullom Voe

Frigg

Flotta
Piper
Beatrice
Nigg Bay
St Fergus
Cruden Bay
Forties

Ekofisk
Auk

North Sea

SCOTLAND

Edinburgh

Sunderland
Gordon
Teesside

Leeds
Scunthorpe
Morecambe
Viking
Sheffield
Immingham
Easington
Ellesmere Port
Theddlethorpe

NORTHERN
IRELAND
Belfast

ENGLAND

Bacton

REPUBLIC
OF
IRELAND

Birmingham
Coventry

WALES

Luton
Dagenham
London

Llanwern
Avonmouth
Swindon
Port Talbot

Fawley

Energy sources
- Oilfield
- Gasfield
- Coalfield
- Oil pipeline
- Gas pipeline

Industry
- Chemicals
- Iron and steel
- Motor vehicles
- Electronics
- $ Financial services

Scale 1 : 5 000 000

WWW National Statistics Online
www.statistics.gov.uk
The Department of Trade and Industry
www.dti.gov.uk

This is an image of central London that uses false colours. These colours are used to highlight important features. So for example the river Thames stands out as a purple line. The Thames flows from Barnes in the south western corner to Docklands in the north eastern corner. This satellite image covers an area of 250 sq km.

1 The rectangular black areas are the old London Docks. This is where ships used to be unloaded. Modern ships are too big for these docks which closed in 1981. Now the whole area is being redeveloped as part of Docklands.

2 The large bends on the river are called meanders. The area inside this meander is called the Isle of Dogs.

3 The centre of London is shown as a large pale purple patch. You can see the road and rail bridges which cross the river Thames.

4 These are the Houses of Parliament.

5 This is Buckingham Palace, with the Palace Gardens, Green Park and St James Park shown in green.

6 The green colours on the image are the parks and open spaces of London. Hyde Park stands out very clearly, with the Serpentine Lake in black. North of this is Regent's Park also shown in green.

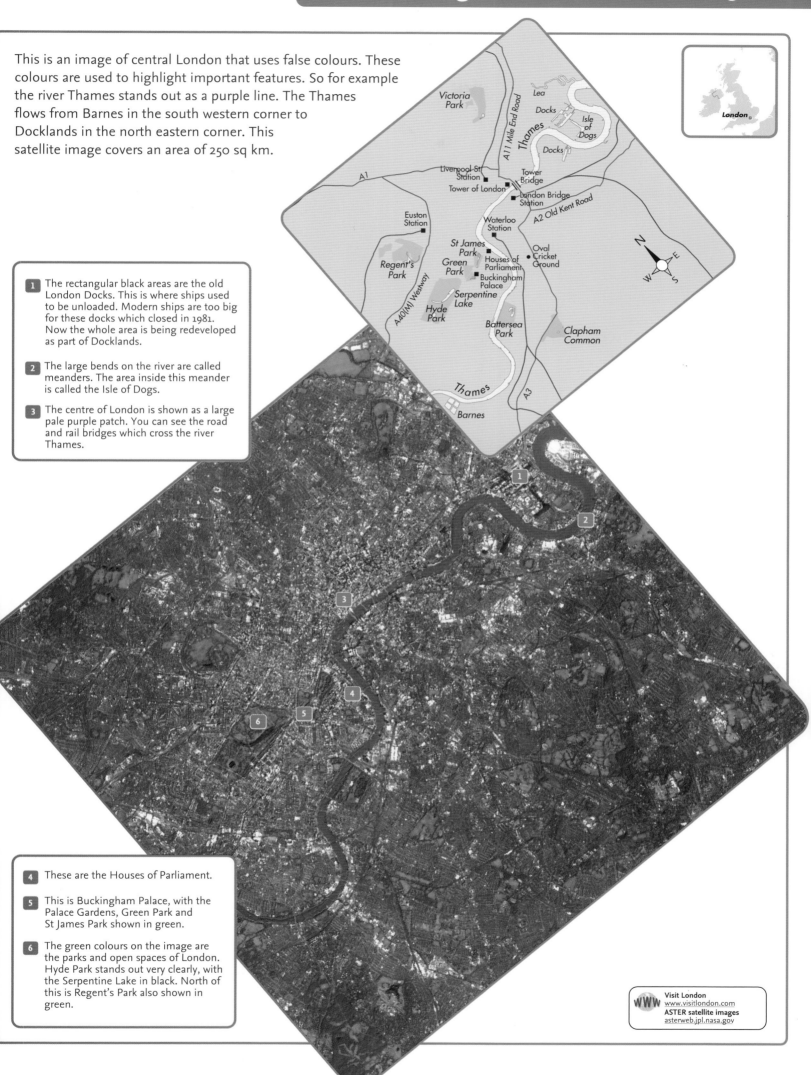

WWW Visit London
www.visitlondon.com
ASTER satellite images
asterweb.jpl.nasa.gov

Key

over 5000 m
3000 – 5000 m
2000 – 3000 m
1000 – 2000 m
500 – 1000 m
200 – 500 m
0 – 200 m
land below sea level

Ice cap

▲ 5642   Mountain height (in metres)

Scale 1 : 25 000 000

0   250   500   750   1000 km

Facts about Europe Relief

Area
9 908 599 sq km

Highest peak
El'brus 5642 m

Lowest point
Caspian Sea -28 m

Longest river
Volga 3 688 km

Largest lake
Caspian Sea 371 000 sq km

Conic Equidistant projection

EUROSTAT
europa.eu.int/comm/eurostat
United Nations Population
Information Network
www.un.org/popin

Key

——	Country boundary
- - -	Disputed boundary
——	Road
——	Railway
·····	Ferry route
✈	Airport
■	Capital city
◉	Large town or city
○	Other town or city

Scale 1 : 25 000 000

0   250   500   750   1000 km

A. ANDORRA
AL. ALBANIA
B.-H. BOSNIA-HERZEGOVINA
L. LIECHTENSTEIN
LUX. LUXEMBOURG
M. MONACO
MAC. MACEDONIA
MON. MONTENEGRO
NETH. NETHERLANDS
R.F. RUSSIAN FEDERATION
S.M. SAN MARINO
SER. SERBIA
SWITZ. SWITZERLAND

Facts about Europe Political

Population*
582 000 000

Largest City
Paris 9 854 000

Largest Country*
Ukraine 603 700 sq km

Country with most people*
Germany 82 476 000

*excluding European Russian Federation

Conic Equidistant projection

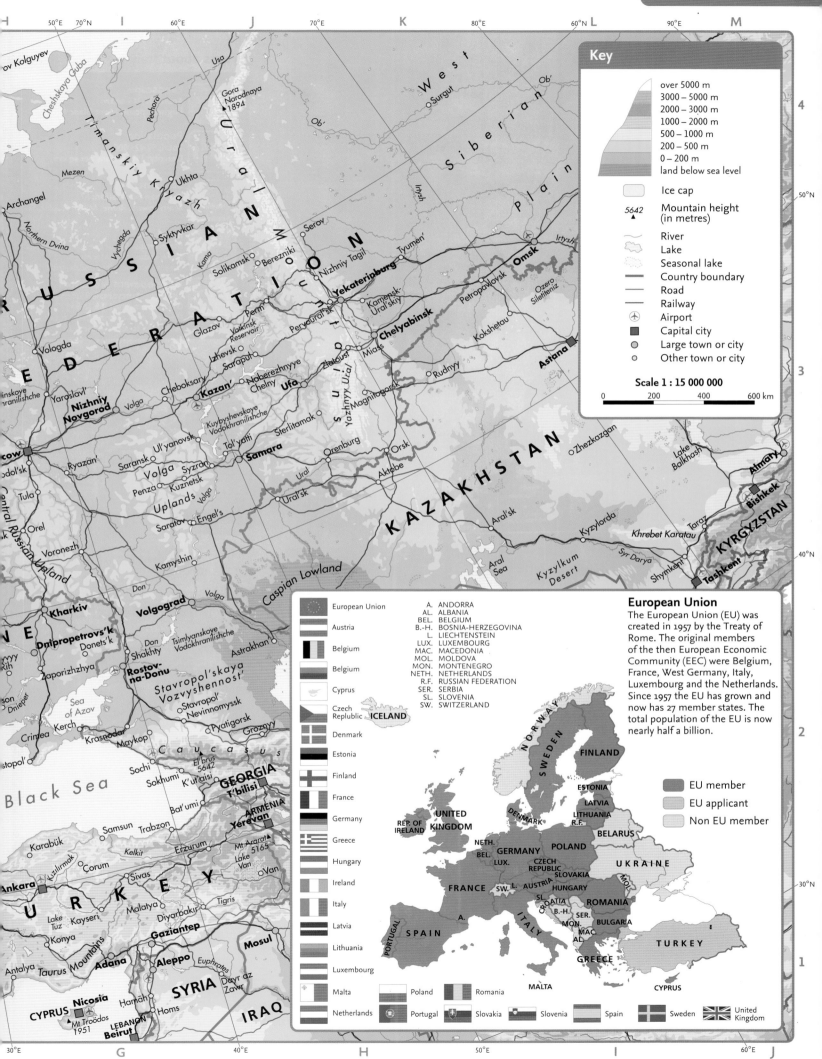

Conic Equidistant projection

Landscape
Area: 301 245 sq km
Highest point: Mont Blanc 4808 m

Population
Total: 57 423 000
Density: 191 persons per sq km

Settlement
% Urban population: 67
Main towns: Rome, Milan, Naples, Turin

Land use
Main crops: Sugar beets, corn, grapes
Main industries: Machinery, metal products, chemicals, food

Development indicators
Life expectancy: male 75, female 81
GNP per capita: US$ 18 960
Primary school enrolment ratio: 100
% Access to safe water: 100

Key

over 5000 m	River
3000 – 5000 m	Lake
2000 – 3000 m	Country boundary
1000 – 2000 m	Road
500 – 1000 m	Railway
200 – 500 m	Ferry
0 – 200 m	Airport
land below sea level	Capital city
Mountain height (in metres)	Large town or city
Ice cap	Other town or city

4808 ▲ Mountain height (in metres)

Scale 1 : 5 250 000

0   50   100   150   200 km

Lambert Conformal Conic projection

Annual rainfall

Heaviest rainfall occurs during autumn and winter when westerly winds blow against the Alps and Apennines. Lowlands in the north and east have less rainfall because they are sheltered. The south has very little rainfall in summer.

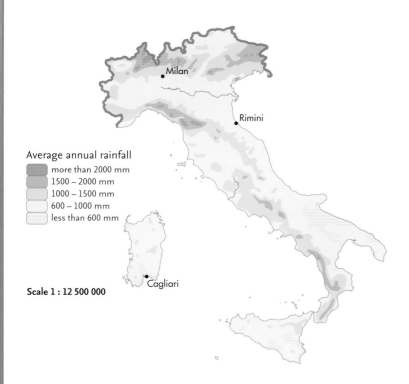

Average annual rainfall

- more than 2000 mm
- 1500 – 2000 mm
- 1000 – 1500 mm
- 600 – 1000 mm
- less than 600 mm

Scale 1 : 12 500 000

Climate statistics

The climate of Italy is greatly influenced by relief. The northern and central uplands have lower temperatures. Rainfall is higher to the west of the Apennines than to the east. Winters become milder and summers become hotter and drier as you move further south.

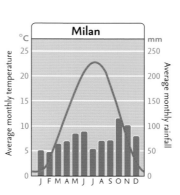

Milan	Jan	Feb	Mar	Apr	May	Jun	Jul	Aug	Sep	Oct	Nov	Dec
Temperature - °C	1	3	8	13	17	21	23	22	19	13	7	2
Rainfall - mm	52	49	65	70	85	89	55	71	72	114	101	80

Rimini	Jan	Feb	Mar	Apr	May	Jun	Jul	Aug	Sep	Oct	Nov	Dec
Temperature - °C	3	6	9	14	18	21	24	24	20	15	9	6
Rainfall - mm	64	36	68	71	57	57	71	61	61	93	114	79

Cagliari	Jan	Feb	Mar	Apr	May	Jun	Jul	Aug	Sep	Oct	Nov	Dec
Temperature - °C	10	10	12	15	19	23	25	25	23	18	14	12
Rainfall - mm	54	54	46	29	25	11	4	7	32	61	79	71

Temperature: January

The mountains in the north and the central uplands can have very low temperatures. Northern lowlands are affected by cold winds from Europe. Coastal areas are the warmest.

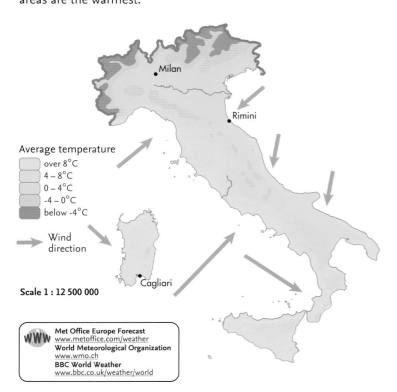

Average temperature

- over 8°C
- 4 – 8°C
- 0 – 4°C
- -4 – 0°C
- below -4°C

→ Wind direction

Scale 1 : 12 500 000

WWW Met Office Europe Forecast
www.metoffice.com/weather
World Meteorological Organization
www.wmo.ch
BBC World Weather
www.bbc.co.uk/weather/world

Temperature: July

Sheltered northern lowlands and coastal areas have hot summers. Other areas are cooler due to their altitude. In the south, hot, dry winds from Africa can lead to very high temperatures.

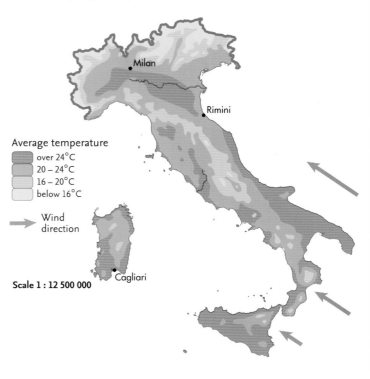

Average temperature

- over 24°C
- 20 – 24°C
- 16 – 20°C
- below 16°C

→ Wind direction

Scale 1 : 12 500 000

National Parks and Protected Areas have been created in Italy to preserve wildlife and natural vegetation. Most of these areas are inland and despite its long coastline, Italy has very few protected coastal areas. Pollution from oil spillage and industrial waste remains around the coast for long periods due to the low tidal movements of the Mediterranean Sea.

Ferret Valley near Mont Blanc

Air pollutants

As in other developed countries it is in the main industrial areas of Italy that most harmful substances such as oxides of sulphur and nitrogen are released into the atmosphere. The main sources of these pollutants are power stations and car exhausts.

Sources of pollutants
- Fuels and energy production
- Energy combustion
- Oil refining
- Manufacturing industries
- Road transport

Sulphur oxides
4%
6%
7%
26%
57%

Nitrous oxides
28%
7%
2%
8%
55%

WWW
National Institute of Statistics
www.istat.it
EUROSTAT
europa.eu.int/comm/eurostat
The Italian Park Portal
www.parks.it

Mont Blanc 4808

Lake Maggiore

Lake Como

Stelvio National Park

Dolomiti Bellunesi National Park

Piave

Trieste

Gran Paradiso National Park

Milan

Lake Garda

Adda

Oglio

Venice

Adige

Gulf of Venice

Turin

Po

Tanaro

Po

Parma

Reggio

Modena

Ferrara

Bologna

Genoa

Reno

Rimini

Gulf of Genoa

Florence

Monte Falterona National Park

Arno

Ancona

Pisa

Adriatic Sea

L i g u r i a n   S e a

Isola d'Elba

Ombrone

Tiber

Monti Sibillini National Park

Grand Sasso and Monti d. Laga National Park

Pescara

Pescara

Tiber

Maiella National Park

Rome

Abruzzo National Park

Gargano National Park

Arcipelago de la Maddalena National Park

Circeo National Park

Ofanto

Bari

Olbia

Naples

Vesuvius ▲1281
Vesuvius National Park

Bradano

Brindisi

Pontine Is

Taranto

Tirso

Golfo di Orosei Gennargentu e Asinara National Park

Cliento and Diano National Park

Pollino National Park

Gulf of Taranto

Oristano

Sardinia

Cagliari

T y r r h e n i a n   S e a

Calabria National Parks

I o n i a n   S e a

Isole Lipari

Aspromonte National Park

Palermo

Reggio di Calabria

Mt Etna 3323 ▲

Catania

S i c i l y

Gela

Siracusa

Isola di Pantelleria

Areas at risk from industrial pollution

Coastal areas most at risk from oil pollution

Main tourist area

National Park

Protected Area

Scale 1 : 5 000 000

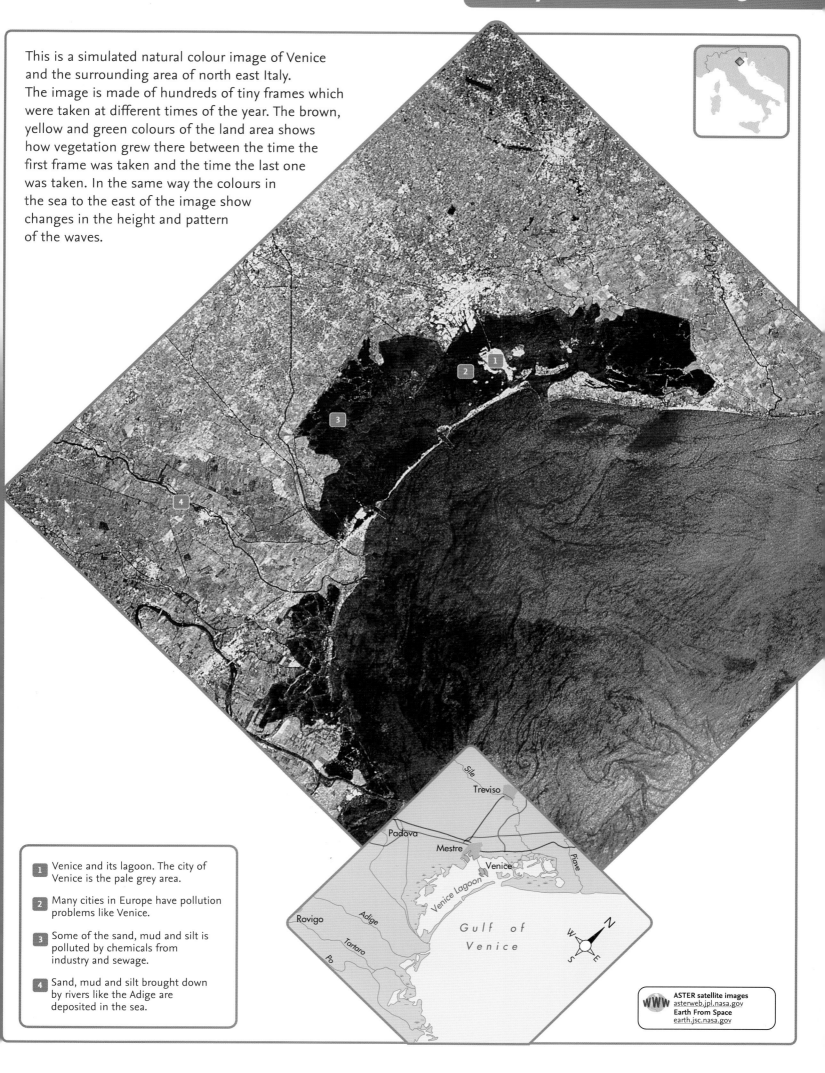

This is a simulated natural colour image of Venice and the surrounding area of north east Italy. The image is made of hundreds of tiny frames which were taken at different times of the year. The brown, yellow and green colours of the land area shows how vegetation grew there between the time the first frame was taken and the time the last one was taken. In the same way the colours in the sea to the east of the image show changes in the height and pattern of the waves.

1 Venice and its lagoon. The city of Venice is the pale grey area.

2 Many cities in Europe have pollution problems like Venice.

3 Some of the sand, mud and silt is polluted by chemicals from industry and sewage.

4 Sand, mud and silt brought down by rivers like the Adige are deposited in the sea.

Sile

Treviso

Padova

Mestre

Venice

Piave

Rovigo

Adige

Venice Lagoon

Tartaro

Po

Gulf of Venice

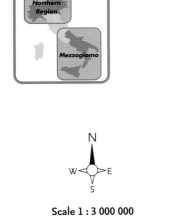

Northern Region

Mezzogiorno

N
W—E
S

Scale 1 : 3 000 000

0   40   80   120 km

Key

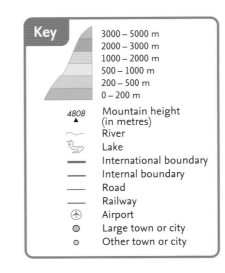

3000 – 5000 m
2000 – 3000 m
1000 – 2000 m
500 – 1000 m
200 – 500 m
0 – 200 m

4808 ▲ Mountain height (in metres)
~ River
Lake
—— International boundary
—— Internal boundary
—— Road
—— Railway
✈ Airport
◉ Large town or city
○ Other town or city

Facts about Northern Italy

Landscape
Area: 97 756 sq km
Highest point: Mont Blanc 4808 m

Population
Total: 21 752 576
Density: 223 persons per sq km

Settlement
Main towns: Milan, Turin, Genoa

Land use
Main crops: Cereals, rice
Main industries: Electrical goods, cars

WWW **National Institute of Statistics**
www.istat.it

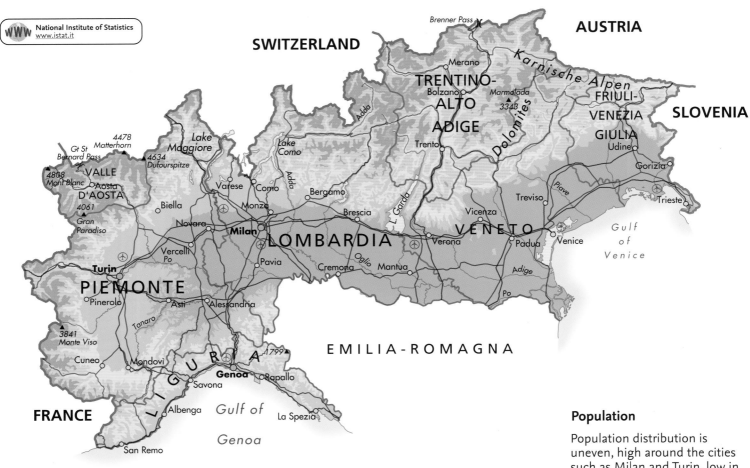

Land use

The main industrial cities are in the west of the region. The fertile lowlands in the Po Valley produce wheat, maize and rice.

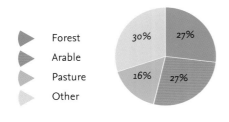

Forest
Arable
Pasture
Other

30%   27%
16%   27%

Employment

The manufacture of consumer goods, especially cars and car components, dominates the region's economy.

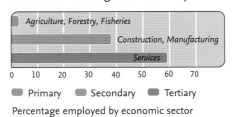

Agriculture, Forestry, Fisheries
Construction, Manufacturing
Services

0 10 20 30 40 50 60 70

■ Primary ■ Secondary ■ Tertiary

Percentage employed by economic sector

Population

Population distribution is uneven, high around the cities such as Milan and Turin, low in the mountains.

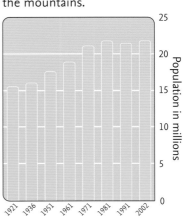

Population in millions

25
20
15
10
5
0

1921 1936 1951 1961 1971 1981 1991 2002

Lambert Conformal Conic projection

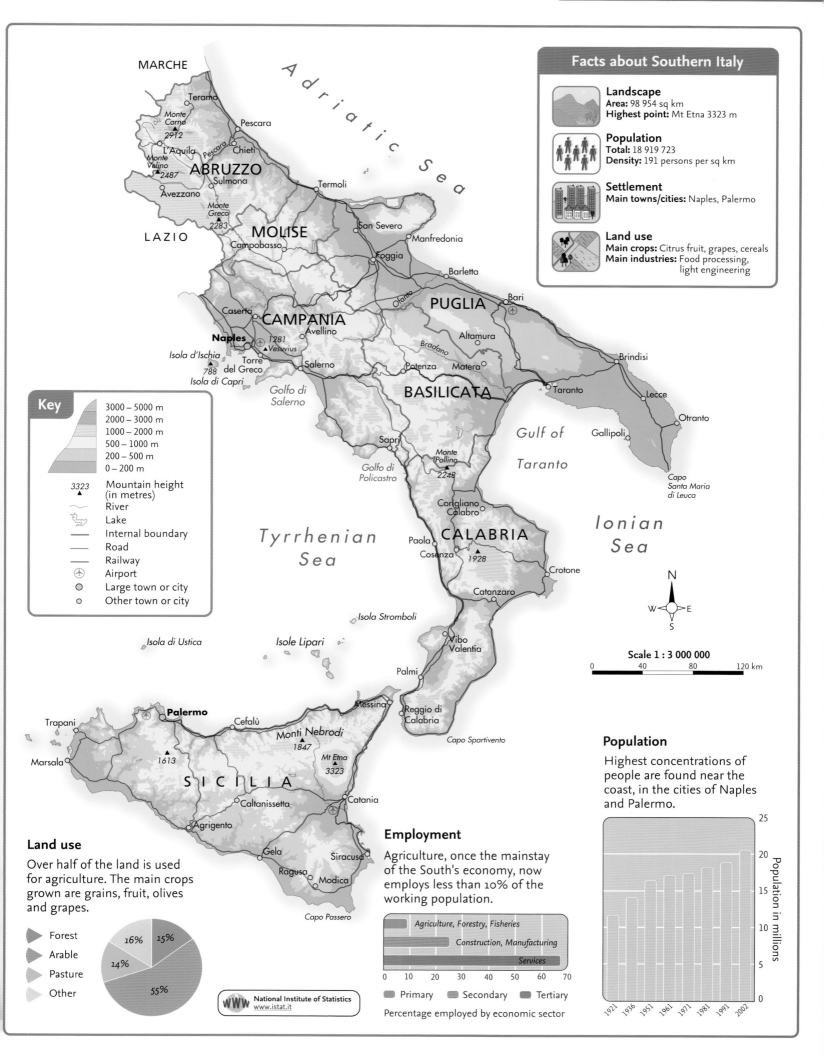

MARCHE

Adriatic Sea

Teramo
Monte Corno 2912
Pescara
L'Aquila
Pescara
Chieti
Monte Velino 2487
ABRUZZO
Sulmona
Avezzano
Monte Greco 2283
MOLISE
Termoli
LAZIO
Campobasso
San Severo
Manfredonia
Foggia
Barletta
Caserta
CAMPANIA
PUGLIA
Bari
Avellino
Altamura
Braciano
Brindisi
Naples
1281 Vesuvius
Isola d'Ischia
Torre del Greco
788
Salerno
Potenza
Matera
Lecce
Isola di Capri
Golfo di Salerno
BASILICATA
Taranto
Otranto
Sapri
Gallipoli
Golfo di Policastro
Monte Pollino 2248
Gulf of Taranto
Capo Santa Maria di Leuca
Corigliano Calabro
Ionian Sea
Paola
CALABRIA
Cosenza
1928
Crotone
Tyrrhenian Sea
Catanzaro
Isola Stromboli
Isole Lipari
Isola di Ustica
Vibo Valentia
Palmi
Messina
Reggio di Calabria
Capo Spartivento
Trapani
Palermo
Cefalù
Monti Nebrodi 1847
Mt Etna 3323
Marsala
1613
Caltanissetta
SICILIA
Catania
Agrigento
Gela
Siracusa
Ragusa
Modica
Capo Passero

Facts about Southern Italy

Landscape
Area: 98 954 sq km
Highest point: Mt Etna 3323 m

Population
Total: 18 919 723
Density: 191 persons per sq km

Settlement
Main towns/cities: Naples, Palermo

Land use
Main crops: Citrus fruit, grapes, cereals
Main industries: Food processing, light engineering

Key

3000 – 5000 m
2000 – 3000 m
1000 – 2000 m
500 – 1000 m
200 – 500 m
0 – 200 m

3323 ▲ Mountain height (in metres)
River
Lake
Internal boundary
Road
Railway
Airport
Large town or city
Other town or city

Scale 1 : 3 000 000

0   40   80   120 km

N
W   E
S

Land use

Over half of the land is used for agriculture. The main crops grown are grains, fruit, olives and grapes.

- Forest
- Arable
- Pasture
- Other

16% 15% 14% 55%

National Institute of Statistics
www.istat.it

Employment

Agriculture, once the mainstay of the South's economy, now employs less than 10% of the working population.

Agriculture, Forestry, Fisheries
Construction, Manufacturing
Services

0 10 20 30 40 50 60 70

Primary   Secondary   Tertiary

Percentage employed by economic sector

Population

Highest concentrations of people are found near the coast, in the cities of Naples and Palermo.

Population in millions

25
20
15
10
5
0

1921 1936 1951 1961 1971 1981 1991 2002

Lambert Conformal Conic projection

Key

- over 5000 m
- 3000 – 5000 m
- 2000 – 3000 m
- 1000 – 2000 m
- 500 – 1000 m
- 200 – 500 m
- 0 – 200 m
- land below sea level

Ice cap

▲ 8848 Mountain height (in metres)

Scale 1 : 40 000 000

0   500   1000   1500 km

ARCTIC OCEAN

EUROPE

Alps
Carpathian Mts
Danube
Vistula
Baltic Sea
Lake Ladoga
Lake Onega
North European Plain
North Cape
Kola Peninsula
Barents Sea
Spitsbergen
Novaya Zemlya
Zemlya Frantsa-Iosifa
Severnaya Zemlya
New Siberia Islands
Wrangel Island
Khrebet Kolymskiy

Taymyr Peninsula
Laptev Sea

Central Russian Uplands
Volga
Don
Ural Mountains
Ob'
West Siberian Plain
Yenisey
Narodnaya 1894

Central Siberian Plateau
Nizhnyaya Tunguska
Lena
Verkhoyanskiy Khrebet
Khrebet Dzhugdzhur
Sea of Okhotsk

Black Sea
Caucasus
Mount Ararat 5165 ▲
Taurus Mts
Lake Van
Lake Urmia
Caspian Sea
Elburz Mts
Aral Sea
Syr Darya
Lake Balkhash
Irtysh
Ob'
Lake Zaysan
Yenisey
Altai Mountains
Lake Baikal
Stanovoy Khrebet
Amur
Da Hinggan Ling
Manchuria

Dead Sea
Euphrates
Tigris
Zagros Mountains
Dasht-e Kavir
The Gulf
Amu Darya
Tien Shan
Tarim Basin
K2 8611 ▲
Kunlun Shan
Plateau of Tibet
Gobi Desert
Huang He
Bo Hai
North China Plain
Yellow Sea

An Nafūd
Hijaz
Arabian Peninsula
'Asīr
Rub' al Khālī
Gulf of Oman
Makran
Helmand
Hindu Kush
Karakoram Ra.
Indus
Sulaiman Range
Sutlej
Himalaya
Annapurna 8091 ▲
Mount Everest ▲ 8848
Gongga Shan 7514 ▲
Chang Jiang
Nan Ling

Jazīrat Maṣīrah
Thar Desert
Narmada
Ganges
Brahmaputra
Mouths of the Ganges
Irrawaddy
Xi Jiang

Socotra
Arabian Sea
Western Ghats
Deccan
Eastern Ghats
Bay of Bengal
Mouths of the Irrawaddy
Hainan
Luzon
Luzon Strait
Taiwan
East China Sea
Okinawa

Laccadive Islands
Sri Lanka
Andaman Islands
Andaman Sea
Mekong
South China Sea
Philippines
Palawan
Sulu Sea
Celebes Sea

Maldives
Nicobar Islands
Gulf of Thailand
Peninsular Malaysia
Strait of Malacca

Chagos Archipelago
INDIAN OCEAN
Kepulauan Mentawai
Sumatra
Borneo
Java Sea
Celebes

Java
Bali
Lombok
Flores

N
W   E
S

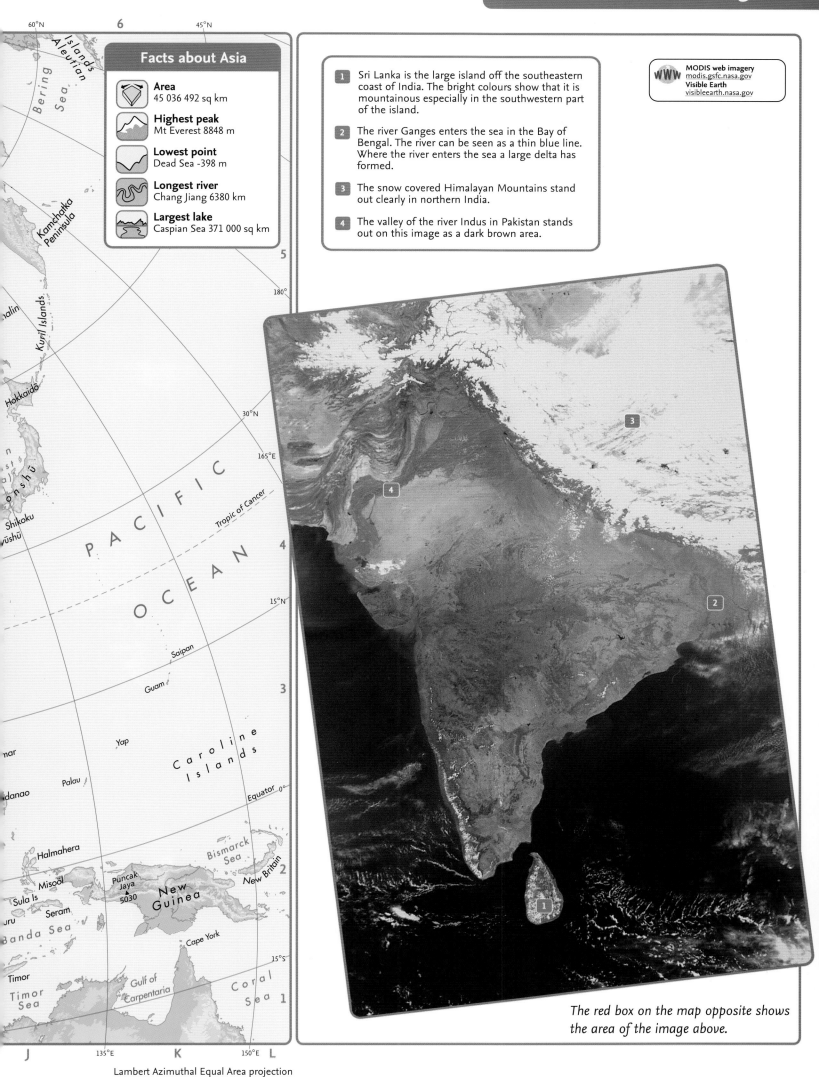

Facts about Asia

Area
45 036 492 sq km

Highest peak
Mt Everest 8848 m

Lowest point
Dead Sea -398 m

Longest river
Chang Jiang 6380 km

Largest lake
Caspian Sea 371 000 sq km

1 Sri Lanka is the large island off the southeastern coast of India. The bright colours show that it is mountainous especially in the southwestern part of the island.

2 The river Ganges enters the sea in the Bay of Bengal. The river can be seen as a thin blue line. Where the river enters the sea a large delta has formed.

3 The snow covered Himalayan Mountains stand out clearly in northern India.

4 The valley of the river Indus in Pakistan stands out on this image as a dark brown area.

WWW **MODIS web imagery**
modis.gsfc.nasa.gov
Visible Earth
visibleearth.nasa.gov

The red box on the map opposite shows the area of the image above.

Lambert Azimuthal Equal Area projection

Key

- over 5000 m
- 3000 – 5000 m
- 2000 – 3000 m
- 1000 – 2000 m
- 500 – 1000 m
- 200 – 500 m
- 0 – 200 m
- land below sea level
- Ice cap
- 8848 ▲ Mountain height (in metres)
- River
- Seasonal river
- Lake
- Seasonal lake
- Country boundary
- Disputed boundary
- Road
- Railway
- ✈ Airport
- ■ Capital city
- ● Large town or city
- ○ Other town or city

Scale 1 : 20 000 000

0   200   400   600   800 km

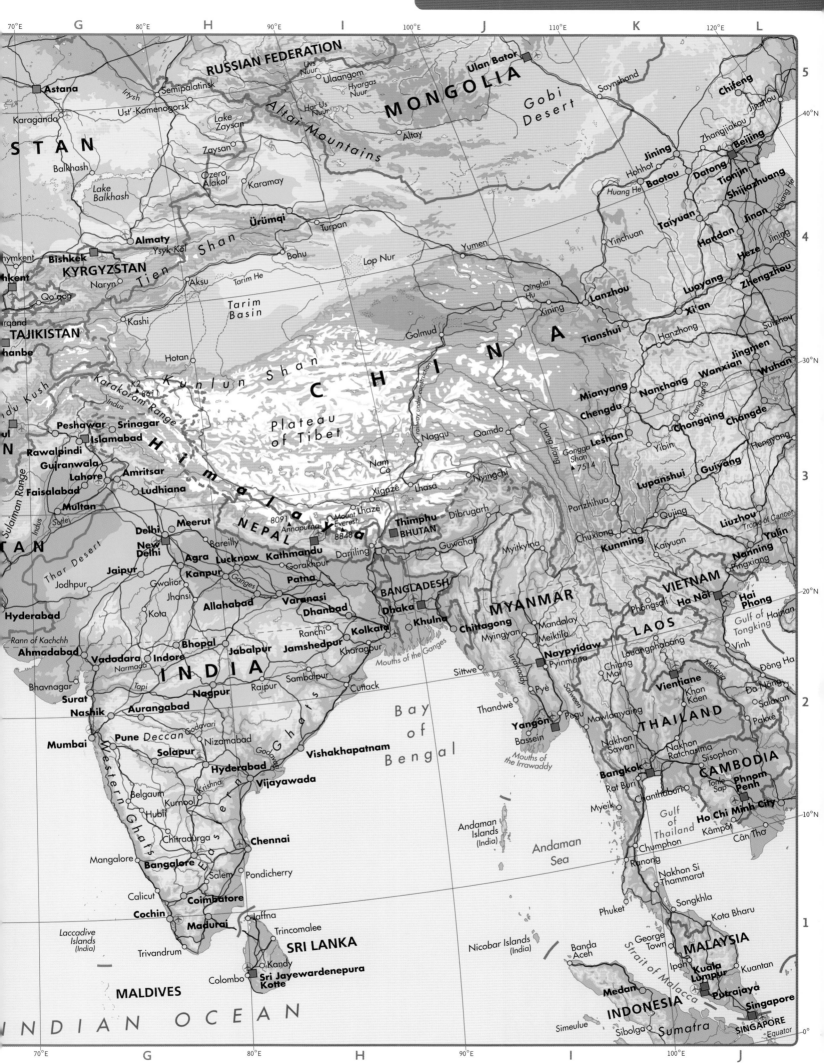

RUSSIAN FEDERATION

Astana
Karaganda
Balkhash
Lake Balkhash

Semipalatinsk
Ust'-Kamenogorsk
Ozero Alakol'
Lake Zaysan
Zaysan

Irtysh

MONGOLIA
Ulan Bator
Ulaangom
Uvs Nuur
Hyargas Nuur
Har Us Nuur
Altay
Saynshand

Gobi Desert

Chifeng
Zhangjiakou
Beijing

Altai Mountains

STAN
Ürümqi
Tien Shan
Ysyk-Köl
Almaty
Bishkek
KYRGYZSTAN
hkent
nymkent
Naryn
Qo'qon
rgand
TAJIKISTAN
hanbe

Turpan
Bohu
Lop Nur
Karamay
Aksu
Kashi
Tarim He
Hotan

Tarim Basin

Yumen
Qinghai Hu
Golmud
Xining
Lanzhou
Tianshui
Xi'an
Luoyang
Zhengzhou
Yinchuan
Hohhot
Jining
Baotou
Taiyuan
Handan
Datong
Tianjin
Shijiazhuang
Jinan
Heze
Jining

Suizhou
Hanzhong
Wuhan
Jingmen
Mianyang
Nanchong
Wanxian
Chengdu
Chongqing
Changde
Hengyang
Yibin
Leshan
Chang Jiang

Kunlun Shan

C H I N A

Plateau of Tibet
Nagqu
Qamdo
Nyingchi
Xigazê
Lhasa
Nam Co
Lhaze
Mount Everest 8848
8091

du Kush
K2 8611
Karakoram Range
Himalaya
Indus
Peshawar
Srinagar
Islamabad
Rawalpindi
Gujranwala
Lahore
Amritsar
Faisalabad
Ludhiana
Multan
Sulaiman Range
Sutlej
NEPAL
Annapurna
Kathmandu
Gorakhpur
Darjiling
Dibrugarh
Thimphu
BHUTAN
Guwahati
Myitkyina
Chuxiong
Kunming
Kaiyuan
Panzhihua
Quijing
Lupanshui
Guiyang
Liuzhou
Yulin
Nanning
Pingxiang
Phongsali
VIETNAM

Kunming

TAN
Delhi
Meerut
New Delhi
Bareilly
Agra
Lucknow
Kanpur
Jhansi
Gwalior
Jaipur
Jodhpur
Kota
Thar Desert
Hyderabad
Rann of Kachchh
Ahmadabad
Vadodara
Indore
Bhopal
Jabalpur
Bhavnagar
Surat
Nashik
Narmada
Tapi
INDIA
Nagpur
Aurangabad
Mumbai
Pune
Deccan
Solapur
Belgaum
Hubli
Hyderabad
Vijayawada
Krishna
Kurnool
Chitradurga
Mangalore
Bangalore
Salem
Calicut
Coimbatore
Cochin
Madurai
Trivandrum
Jaffna
Trincomalee
SRI LANKA
Kandy
Colombo
Sri Jayewardenepura Kotte

Ganges
Patna
Varanasi
Allahabad
Dhanbad
Ranchi
Jamshedpur
Kharagpur
Sambalpur
Raipur
Cuttack
Nizamabad
Godavari
Godavari
Vishakhapatnam
Chennai
Pondicherry
Western Ghats
Eastern Ghats

BANGLADESH
Dhaka
Khulna
Kolkata
Chittagong
Mouths of the Ganges

MYANMAR
Mandalay
Myingyan
Meiktila
Naypyidaw
Pyinmana
Pyè
Sittwe
Thandwè
Yangôn
Bassein
Pegu
Mawlamyaing
Mouths of the Irrawaddy
Irrawaddy
Salween

Bay of Bengal

LAOS
Louangphabang
Chiang Mai
Vientiane
Khon Kaen
Nakhon Sawan
Chiang Rai
THAILAND
Rat Buri
Bangkok
Chanthaburi
Nakhon Ratchasima
Sisophon
CAMBODIA
Tonle Sap
Phnom Penh
Myeik
Ho Chi Minh City
Kâmpôt
Cân Tho
Chumphon
Ranong
Nakhon Si Thammarat
Gulf of Thailand
Phuket
Songkhla
Kota Bharu
George Town
Ipoh
Kuala Lumpur
Kuantan
MALAYSIA
Medan
Putrajaya
Singapore
INDONESIA
Simeulue
Sibolga
Sumatra
SINGAPORE
Banda Aceh
Strait of Malacca

Ha Nôi
Hai Phong
Gulf of Hainan Tongking
Vinh
Đông Ha
Đà Nang
Salavan
Pakxe
Mekong

Tropic of Cancer

Andaman Islands (India)
Andaman Sea
Nicobar Islands (India)

MALDIVES
Laccadive Islands (India)

I N D I A N   O C E A N

Equator

Lambert Azimuthal Equal Area projection

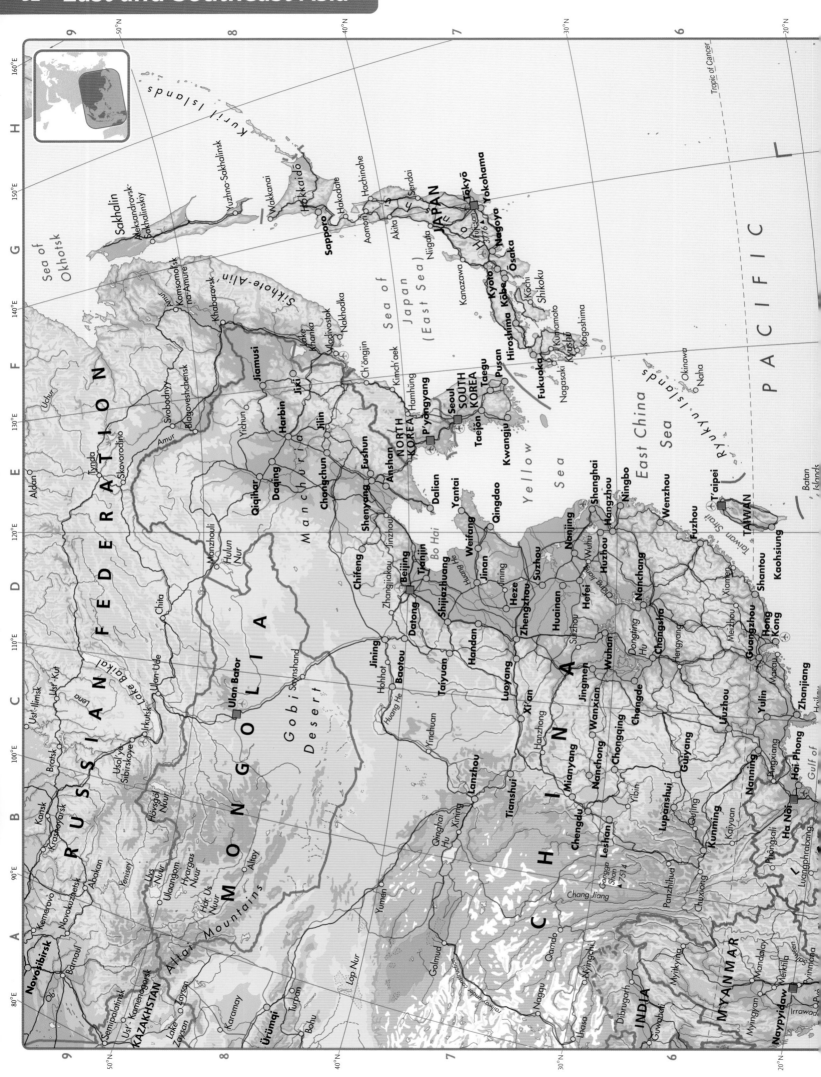

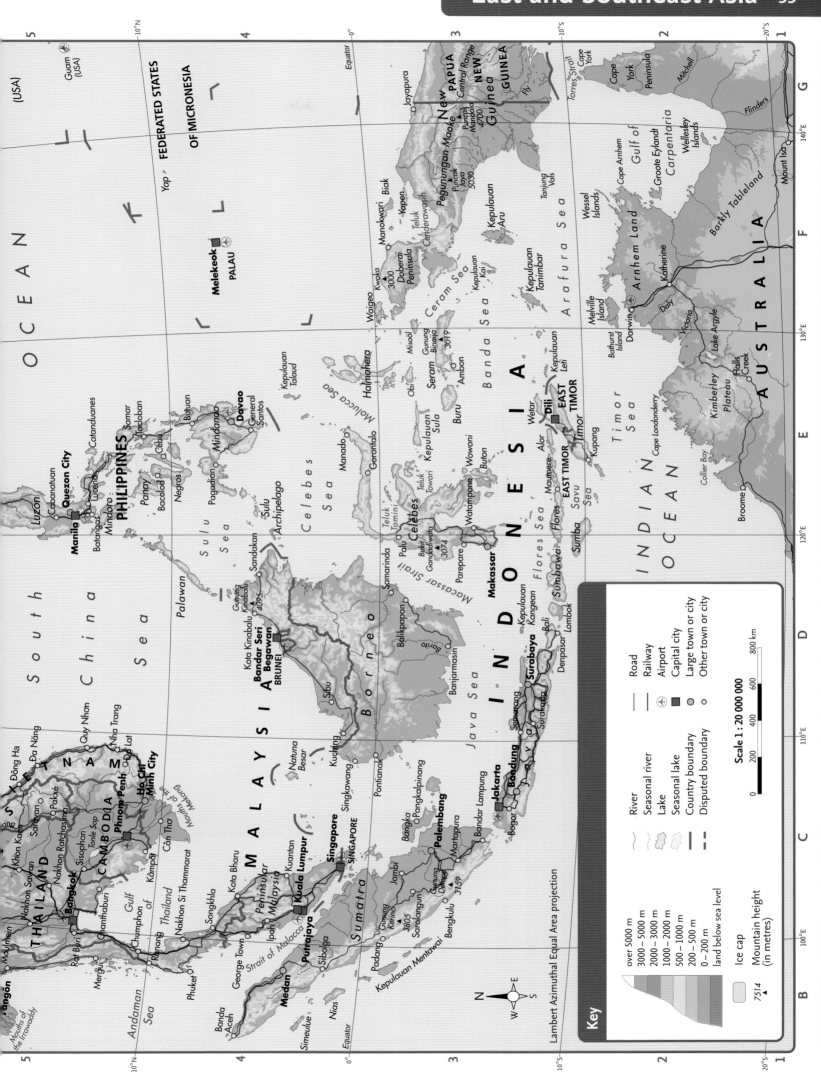

Key

	Road
	Railway
✈	Airport
■	Capital city
○	Large town or city
○	Other town or city

	River
	Seasonal river
	Lake
	Seasonal lake
	Country boundary
	Disputed boundary

Scale 1 : 20 000 000

0   200   400   600   800 km

over 5000 m
3000 – 5000 m
2000 – 3000 m
1000 – 2000 m
500 – 1000 m
200 – 500 m
0 – 200 m
land below sea level

Ice cap

7514 ▲ Mountain height (in metres)

Lambert Azimuthal Equal Area projection

N
W E
S

Facts about Japan

Landscape
Area: 377 727 sq km
Highest point: Fuji-san 3776 m

Population
Total: 127 654 000
Density: 338 persons per sq km

Settlement
% Urban population: 79
Main towns: Tōkyō, Ōsaka-Kōbe, Nagoya, Fukuoka-Kita-Kyūshū

Land use
Main crops: Rice, potatoes, sugar beets
Main industries: Electrical equipment, transport equipment, other machinery, chemicals

Development indicators
Life expectancy: male 77, female 85
GNP per capita: US$ 33 550
Primary school enrolment ratio: 101
% Access to safe water: 100

Key

3000 – 5000 m	
2000 – 3000 m	
1000 – 2000 m	
500 – 1000 m	
200 – 500 m	
0 – 200 m	

3776 ▲ Mountain height (in metres)

～ River
Lake

— Country boundary
--- Disputed boundary
— Road
— Railway
···· Ferry
✈ Airport
■ Capital city
◉ Large town or city
○ Other town or city

Japanese name forms

-dake	peak
-hanto	peninsula
-jima	island
-kai	bay, inlet
-kaikyo	strait
-ko	lake
-nada	sea, gulf
-retto	chain of islands
-san	mountain
-sanchi	mountainous area
-shima	island
-suido	strait, channel
-to	island
-wan	sea
-yama	mountain

Scale 1 : 7 500 000

0   100   200   300   400 km

Albers Equal Area Conic projection

Annual rainfall

The driest parts of Japan are in the north, on the island of Hokkaidō. Most rain falls on the high mountain tops and the southern and western coasts.

Average annual rainfall
- more than 3000 mm
- 2000 – 3000 mm
- 1500 – 2000 mm
- 1000 – 1500 mm
- less than 1000 mm

Scale 1 : 15 000 000

Climate statistics

The tables below list average monthly temperature in degrees centigrade and average monthly rainfall in millimetres for three weather stations in Japan.

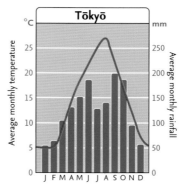

Sapporo	Jan	Feb	Mar	Apr	May	Jun	Jul	Aug	Sep	Oct	Nov	Dec
Temperature - °C	-5	-4	0	6	12	16	20	21	17	11	4	-2
Rainfall - mm	114	92	78	65	59	76	80	131	142	115	104	101

Tōkyō	Jan	Feb	Mar	Apr	May	Jun	Jul	Aug	Sep	Oct	Nov	Dec
Temperature - °C	5	5	8	14	18	22	25	27	23	17	12	7
Rainfall - mm	54	63	102	128	148	181	125	137	193	181	93	56

Kagoshima	Jan	Feb	Mar	Apr	May	Jun	Jul	Aug	Sep	Oct	Nov	Dec
Temperature - °C	7	8	11	16	20	23	27	28	25	20	14	9
Rainfall - mm	95	106	147	256	275	475	323	209	211	108	92	80

Temperature: January

In January temperatures fall below 0°C in the north of Japan. On the south coast and on the southern island of Kyūshū the winter is much milder.

Average temperature
- 4 – 8°C
- 0 – 4°C
- -8 – 0°C
- below -8°C
- → Wind direction

Scale 1 : 15 000 000

Temperature: August

Most of Japan is very warm during the summer, especially in the southern part of the country. Temperatures are cooler on the high mountains in the north.

Average temperature
- over 26°C
- 22 – 26°C
- 18 – 22°C
- below 18°C
- → Wind direction

Scale 1 : 15 000 000

WWW Japan Meteorological Agency
www.jma.go.jp
World Meteorological Organization
www.wmo.ch

Japan is situated on the 'Ring of Fire' around the Pacific Ocean. There are almost 200 volcanoes in the 'Ring of Fire' and over 20 are still active.

Earthquakes are more disastrous than volcanic eruptions in Japan where 5000 earthquakes are recorded annually. The main earthquake zones lie on the Pacific side of Japan. Strong earthquakes may destroy roads and railways, collapse houses and result in many casualties.

Earthquake seismogram :
A seismogram is used to record the horizontal or vertical vibration caused during the course of an earthquake. The vertical divisions represent time intervals of 5 seconds.

Volcanic activity

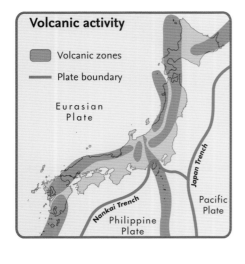

- Volcanic zones
- Plate boundary

Eurasian Plate

Japan Trench

Nankai Trench

Pacific Plate

Philippine Plate

Kōbe earthquake :
In 1995 Kōbe was struck by a huge earthquake which measured 7.1 on the Richter Scale. The centre of the quake was close to the city, caused extensive damage and killed over 5000 people.

- Volcanic rocks
- ▲ Active volcano (erupted since 1850)
- △ Other volcano
- ● Major earthquake

Scale 1 : 9 000 000

Tokachi

Hokkaidō

Sapporo

Usu

Komaga-take

Chōkai

Zao

Honshū

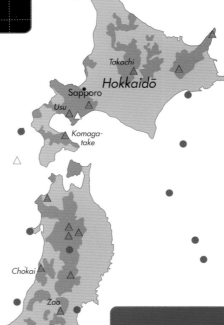

Yake-Dake

Tōkyō

Fuji

Nagoya

Kōbe

Shikoku

Fuji :
Situated on the island of Honshū, Fuji is a dormant volcano which has not erupted since 1707. At 3776 m, it is the highest mountain in Japan and has a crater which is 610 metres in diameter.

Unzen △   △ Aso

Kyūshū

Kagoshima   △ Kirishima

△ Sakurajima

Sakurajima :
Sakurajima is an active volcano situated in Kagoshima Bay. Its eruptions are generally gentle with little explosive activity.

Richter Scale

The scale of measurement used to describe the strength of an earthquake is known as the Richter Scale. The scale measures the energy which is released at the centre of an earthquake. Every year about 50 000 quakes measuring 3 – 4 are recorded worldwide, while only 800 measuring 5 – 6 occur.

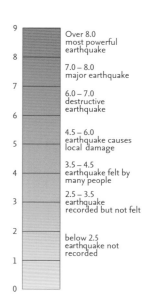

- 9 — Over 8.0 most powerful earthquake
- 8 — 7.0 – 8.0 major earthquake
- 7 — 6.0 – 7.0 destructive earthquake
- 6 —
- 5 — 4.5 – 6.0 earthquake causes local damage
- 4 — 3.5 – 4.5 earthquake felt by many people
- 3 — 2.5 – 3.5 earthquake recorded but not felt
- 2 —
- 1 — below 2.5 earthquake not recorded
- 0 —

WWW USGS National Earthquake Information Center
wwwneic.cr.usgs.gov
Earthquake Research Institute
www.eri.u-tokyo.ac.jp

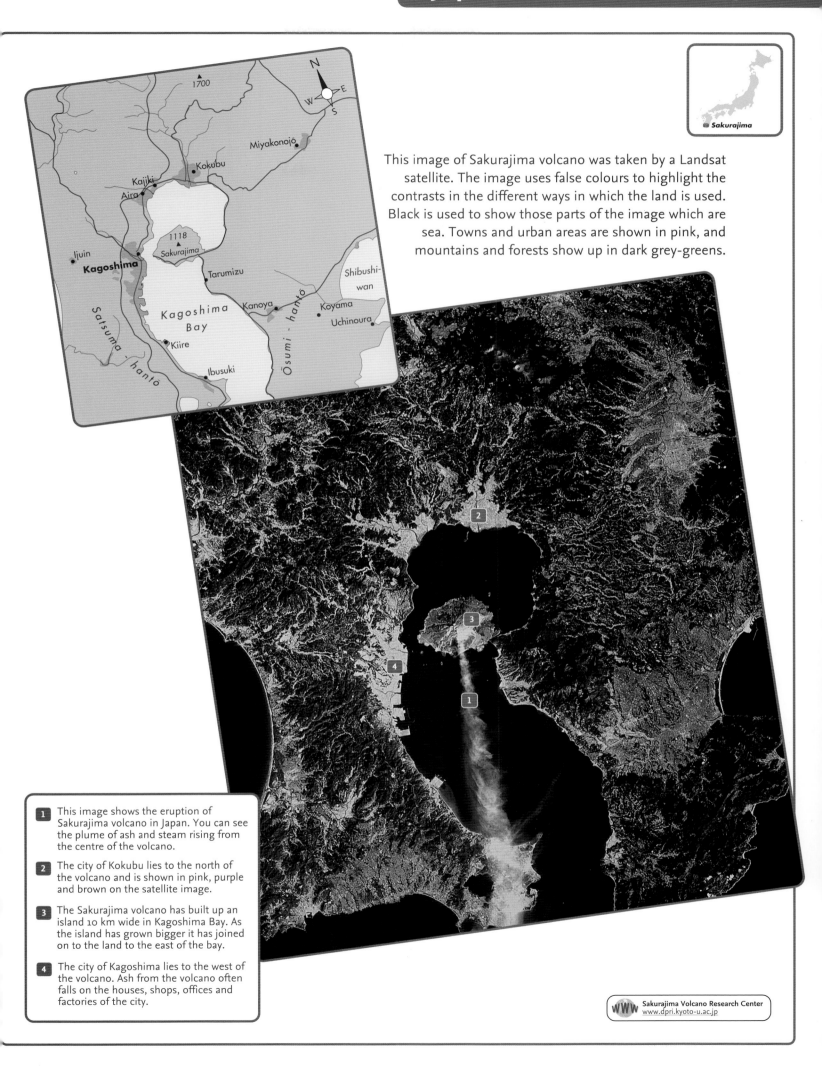

Sakurajima

▲ 1700

Miyakonojō

Kokubu

Kajiki

Aira

Ijuin

Kagoshima

1118 ▲
Sakurajima

Tarumizu

Shibushi-wan

Kanoya

Ōsumi - hantō

Koyama

Uchinoura

Satsuma - hantō

Kagoshima Bay

Kiire

Ibusuki

This image of Sakurajima volcano was taken by a Landsat satellite. The image uses false colours to highlight the contrasts in the different ways in which the land is used. Black is used to show those parts of the image which are sea. Towns and urban areas are shown in pink, and mountains and forests show up in dark grey-greens.

1 This image shows the eruption of Sakurajima volcano in Japan. You can see the plume of ash and steam rising from the centre of the volcano.

2 The city of Kokubu lies to the north of the volcano and is shown in pink, purple and brown on the satellite image.

3 The Sakurajima volcano has built up an island 10 km wide in Kagoshima Bay. As the island has grown bigger it has joined on to the land to the east of the bay.

4 The city of Kagoshima lies to the west of the volcano. Ash from the volcano often falls on the houses, shops, offices and factories of the city.

www Sakurajima Volcano Research Center
www.dpri.kyoto-u.ac.jp

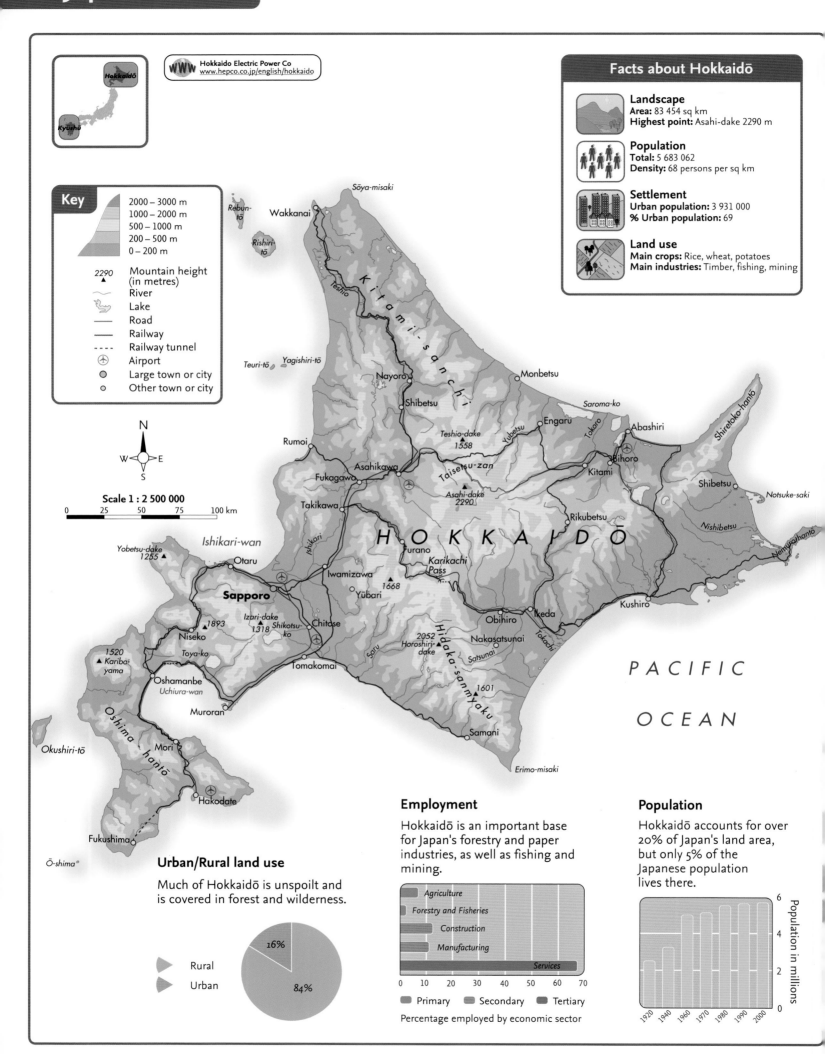

Key

2000 – 3000 m	
1000 – 2000 m	
500 – 1000 m	
200 – 500 m	
0 – 200 m	

2290 ▲ Mountain height (in metres)
〜 River
Lake
—— Road
—— Railway
----- Railway tunnel
⊕ Airport
◉ Large town or city
○ Other town or city

Scale 1 : 2 500 000

0   25   50   75   100 km

Hokkaido Electric Power Co
www.hepco.co.jp/english/hokkaido

Facts about Hokkaidō

Landscape
Area: 83 454 sq km
Highest point: Asahi-dake 2290 m

Population
Total: 5 683 062
Density: 68 persons per sq km

Settlement
Urban population: 3 931 000
% Urban population: 69

Land use
Main crops: Rice, wheat, potatoes
Main industries: Timber, fishing, mining

Urban/Rural land use

Much of Hokkaidō is unspoilt and is covered in forest and wilderness.

16% Rural
84% Urban

Employment

Hokkaidō is an important base for Japan's forestry and paper industries, as well as fishing and mining.

Agriculture
Forestry and Fisheries
Construction
Manufacturing
Services

0   10   20   30   40   50   60   70

■ Primary   ■ Secondary   ■ Tertiary

Percentage employed by economic sector

Population

Hokkaidō accounts for over 20% of Japan's land area, but only 5% of the Japanese population lives there.

Population in millions

1920 1940 1960 1970 1980 1990 2000

Conic Equidistant projection

Facts about Kyūshū

Landscape
Area: 42 170 sq km
Highest point: Kujū-san 1788 m

Population
Total: 13 445 561
Density: 319 persons per sq km

Settlement
Urban population: 7 305 000
% Urban population: 50

Land use
Main crops: Vegetables, rice
Main industries: Car manufacturing, electronics, steel production

Key

1000 – 2000 m
500 – 1000 m
200 – 500 m
0 – 200 m

1788 ▲ Mountain height (in metres)
River
Lake
Road
Railway
⊕ Airport
◯ Large town or city
○ Other town or city

WWW Kyushu Bureau of METI
www.kyushu.meti.go.jp

Scale 1 : 2 500 000
0   25   50   75   100 km

PACIFIC

OCEAN

East China

Sea

Urban/Rural land use

Most of the towns and cities are on the coast. This is also an important rice growing area.

29% Rural
71% Urban

Employment

The electronics and car industries have dominated the island's economy over the last 20 years.

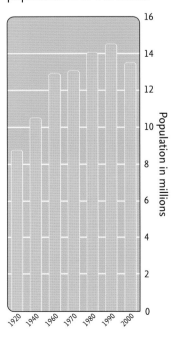

Agriculture
Forestry and Fisheries
Construction
Manufacturing
Services

0 10 20 30 40 50 60 70

Primary   Secondary   Tertiary

Percentage employed by economic sector

Population

The island of Kyūshū is densely populated, the greatest concentration of population is in the north.

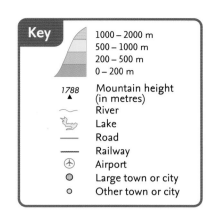

Population in millions

16
14
12
10
8
6
4
2
0

1920 1940 1960 1970 1980 1990 2000

Conic Equidistant projection

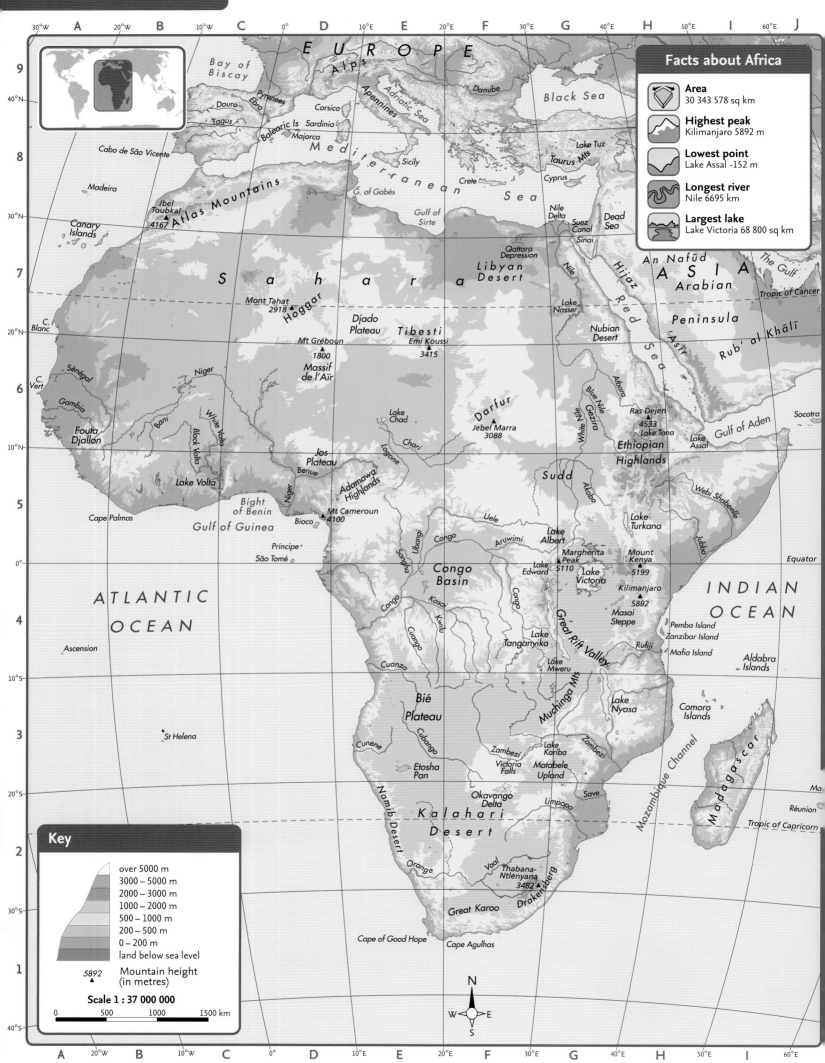

Facts about Africa

Area
30 343 578 sq km

Highest peak
Kilimanjaro 5892 m

Lowest point
Lake Assal -152 m

Longest river
Nile 6695 km

Largest lake
Lake Victoria 68 800 sq km

Key

over 5000 m
3000 – 5000 m
2000 – 3000 m
1000 – 2000 m
500 – 1000 m
200 – 500 m
0 – 200 m
land below sea level

5892 ▲ Mountain height
(in metres)

Scale 1 : 37 000 000
0   500   1000   1500 km

Lambert Azimuthal Equal Area projection

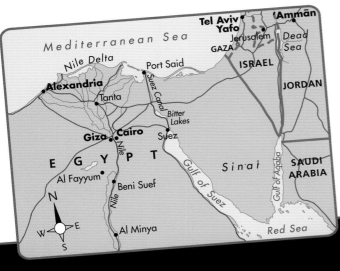

This is an infra-red satellite image of the delta of the river Nile, the Sinai peninsula and the neighbouring parts of Israel, Jordan and Saudi Arabia. Most of this area is desert and this is shown in the pale pinky-brown colour. The red colour in the delta of the river Nile shows that most of the land here is used for farming. The pale blue areas on the edge of the delta are shallow lagoons.

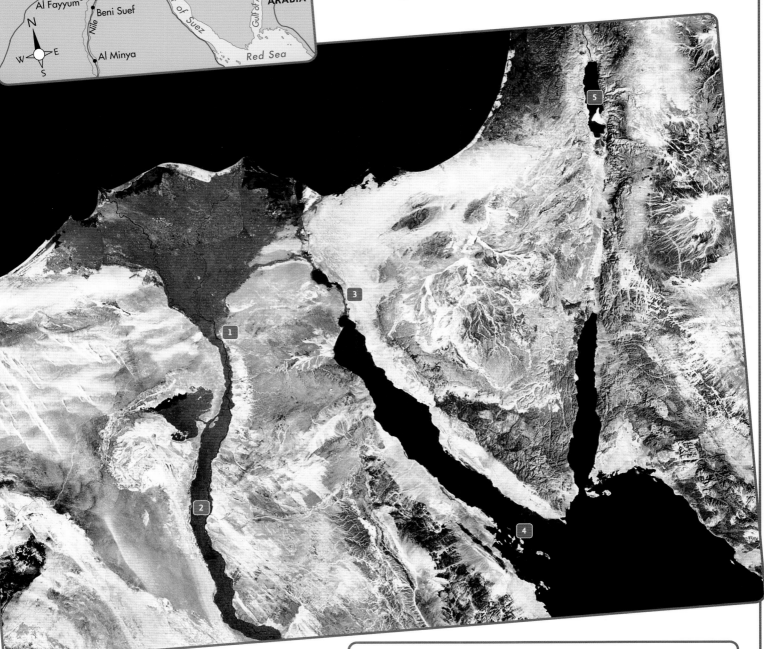

1 The city of Cairo is the dark grey area at the base of the delta.

2 The valley of the river Nile is shown as a dark line which ends at the delta.

3 The Suez Canal was built in 1869 by connecting a series of lakes which are shown in black. The Suez Canal allows ships to sail from the Mediterranean Sea, in the north of the image, to the Red Sea.

4 The Red Sea is shown in black on the image. The pale grey areas in the sea are islands.

5 The Dead Sea in Israel is shown in black on the satellite image.

Visible Earth
visibleearth.nasa.gov

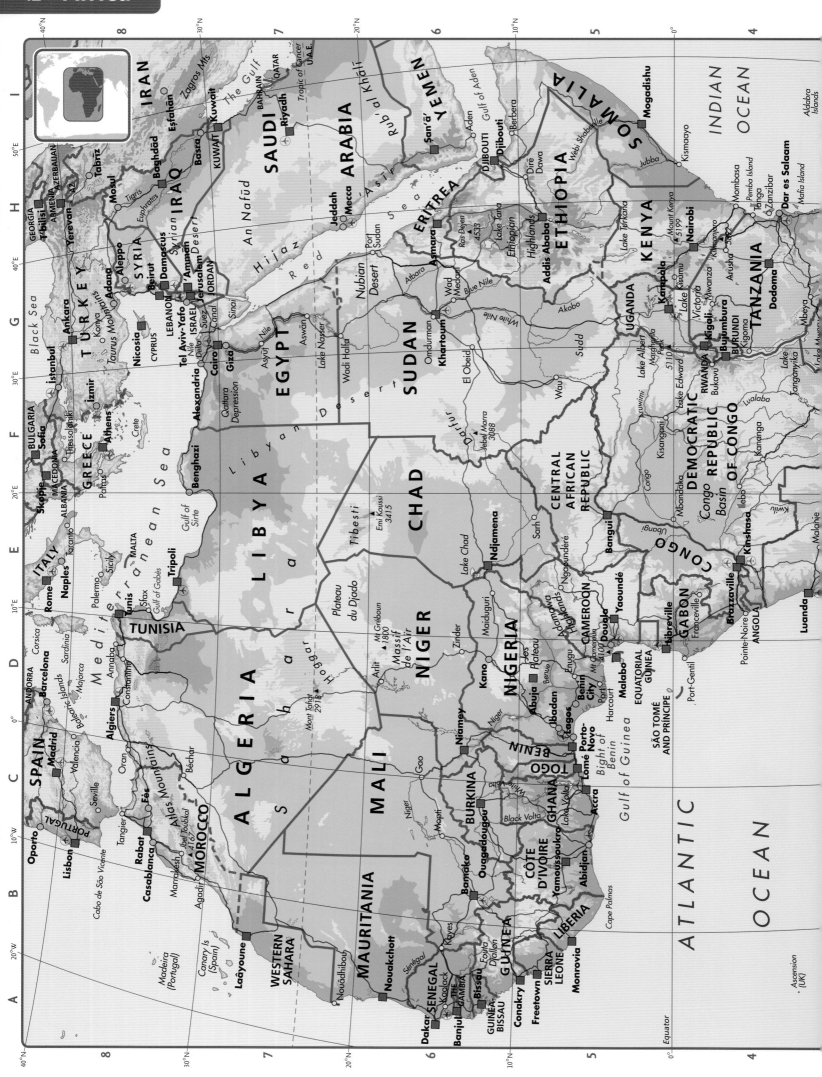

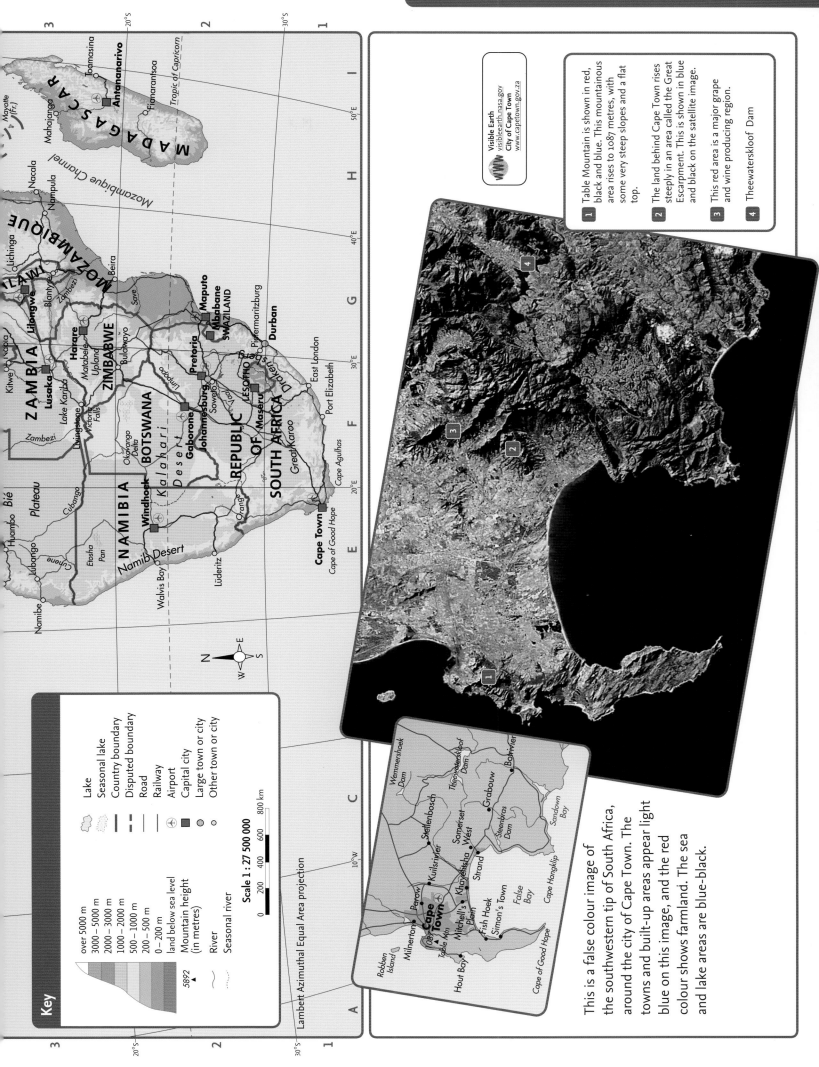

Key

	over 5000 m
	3000–5000 m
	2000–3000 m
	1000–2000 m
	500–1000 m
	200–500 m
	0–200 m
	land below sea level
5892 ▲	Mountain height (in metres)
	River
	Seasonal river

	Lake
	Seasonal lake
	Country boundary
	Disputed boundary
	Road
	Railway
✈	Airport
■	Capital city
●	Large town or city
○	Other town or city

Scale 1 : 27 500 000

0 200 400 600 800 km

Lambert Azimuthal Equal Area projection

Visible Earth
visibleearth.nasa.gov
City of Cape Town
www.capetown.gov.za

1 Table Mountain is shown in red, black and blue. This mountainous area rises to 1087 metres, with some very steep slopes and a flat top.

2 The land behind Cape Town rises steeply in an area called the Great Escarpment. This is shown in blue and black on the satellite image.

3 This red area is a major grape and wine producing region.

4 Theewaterskloof Dam

This is a false colour image of the southwestern tip of South Africa, around the city of Cape Town. The towns and built-up areas appear light blue on this image, and the red colour shows farmland. The sea and lake areas are blue-black.

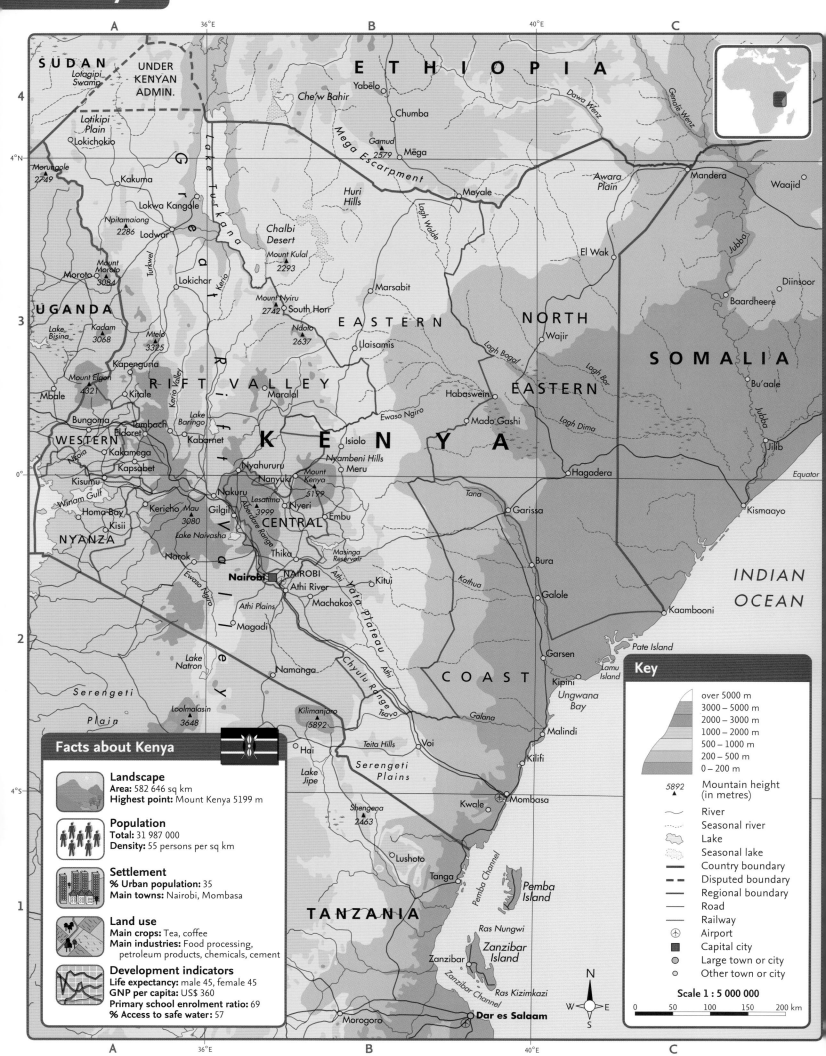

Facts about Kenya

Landscape
Area: 582 646 sq km
Highest point: Mount Kenya 5199 m

Population
Total: 31 987 000
Density: 55 persons per sq km

Settlement
% Urban population: 35
Main towns: Nairobi, Mombasa

Land use
Main crops: Tea, coffee
Main industries: Food processing,
petroleum products, chemicals, cement

Development indicators
Life expectancy: male 45, female 45
GNP per capita: US$ 360
Primary school enrolment ratio: 69
% Access to safe water: 57

Key

over 5000 m
3000 – 5000 m
2000 – 3000 m
1000 – 2000 m
500 – 1000 m
200 – 500 m
0 – 200 m

5892 ▲ Mountain height
(in metres)

River

Seasonal river

Lake

Seasonal lake

Country boundary

Disputed boundary

Regional boundary

Road

Railway

Airport

Capital city

Large town or city

Other town or city

Scale 1 : 5 000 000

0   50   100   150   200 km

Lambert Azimuthal Equal Area projection

Annual rainfall

The heaviest rain falls in April and May. The highlands and western areas receive ample rainfall but most of the north and northeast is very dry.

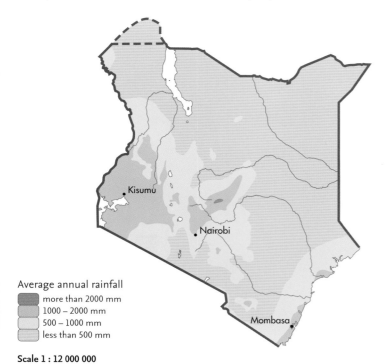

Average annual rainfall
- more than 2000 mm
- 1000 – 2000 mm
- 500 – 1000 mm
- less than 500 mm

Scale 1 : 12 000 000

Climate statistics

Kenya has a tropical climate which varies with altitude. The coastal lowland area is hot and humid but the highlands region is much drier and cooler.

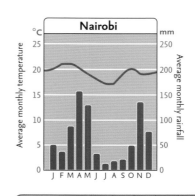

Central Bureau of Statistics
www.cbs.go.ke
Met Office Africa Forecast
www.metoffice.com/weather

Nairobi	Jan	Feb	Mar	Apr	May	Jun	Jul	Aug	Sep	Oct	Nov	Dec
Temperature - °C	20	21	21	20	19	18	17	17	19	20	19	19
Rainfall - mm	49	36	85	153	126	32	13	18	21	48	132	75

Mombasa	Jan	Feb	Mar	Apr	May	Jun	Jul	Aug	Sep	Oct	Nov	Dec
Temperature - °C	28	28	28	28	26	25	24	24	25	26	27	28
Rainfall - mm	17	10	30	108	149	54	34	47	46	62	66	32

Kisumu	Jan	Feb	Mar	Apr	May	Jun	Jul	Aug	Sep	Oct	Nov	Dec
Temperature - °C	24	24	24	23	23	22	22	22	23	24	24	23
Rainfall - mm	62	88	163	207	173	93	63	90	82	72	111	107

Vegetation

Large areas of Kenya are covered in sparsely wooded Savanna. The most varied vegetation is found in the highlands where Savanna gives way to woodland and forest. North of the river Tana semi desert areas support little vegetation.

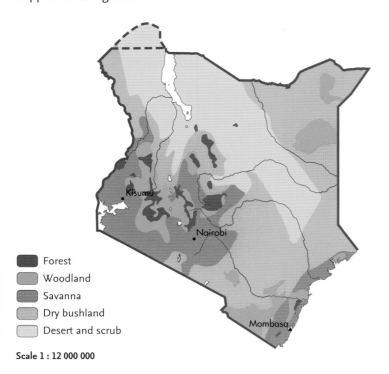

- Forest
- Woodland
- Savanna
- Dry bushland
- Desert and scrub

Scale 1 : 12 000 000

Population

Kenya's population is distributed very unevenly. The most densely populated areas are found in areas with adequate rainfall. The main urban settlements are Nairobi and Mombasa. The dry north and northeast areas are sparsely populated as lack of water limits the development of any settlement.

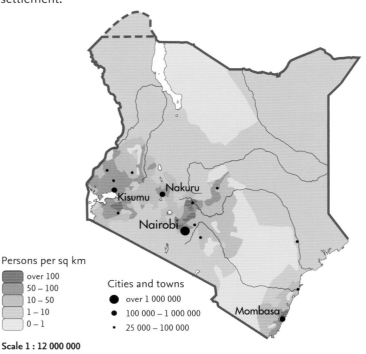

Persons per sq km
- over 100
- 50 – 100
- 10 – 50
- 1 – 10
- 0 – 1

Cities and towns
- over 1 000 000
- 100 000 – 1 000 000
- 25 000 – 100 000

Scale 1 : 12 000 000

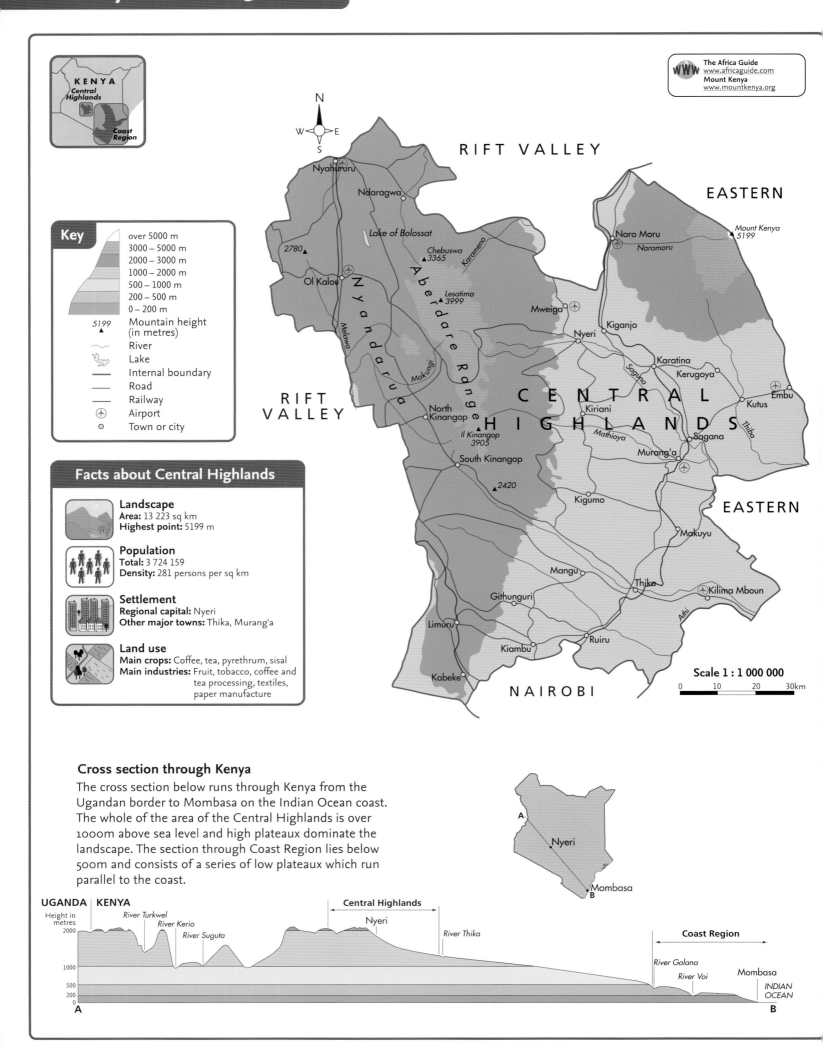

KENYA
Central Highlands
Coast Region

Key

over 5000 m
3000 – 5000 m
2000 – 3000 m
1000 – 2000 m
500 – 1000 m
200 – 500 m
0 – 200 m

5199 ▲ Mountain height (in metres)

~~~ River

Lake

Internal boundary

Road

Railway

Airport

Town or city

Facts about Central Highlands

Landscape
Area: 13 223 sq km
Highest point: 5199 m

Population
Total: 3 724 159
Density: 281 persons per sq km

Settlement
Regional capital: Nyeri
Other major towns: Thika, Murang'a

Land use
Main crops: Coffee, tea, pyrethrum, sisal
Main industries: Fruit, tobacco, coffee and tea processing, textiles, paper manufacture

RIFT VALLEY

EASTERN

Nyahururu
Ndaragwa
Lake of Bolossat
2780 ▲
Chebuswa ▲ 3365
Karamenc
Ol Kalou
Lesatima ▲ 3999
Naro Moru
Mount Kenya ▲ 5199
Naromoru
Mweiga
Kiganjo
Nyeri
Saguna
Karatina
Kerugoya
Embu
North Kinangop
Kiriani
Kutus
Il Kinangop ▲ 3905
Mathioya
Thiba
Sagana
South Kinangop
Murang'a
▲ 2420
Kigumo
Makuyu
Mangu
Thika
Kilima Mboun
Githunguri
Athi
Limuru
Ruiru
Kiambu
Kabeke

RIFT VALLEY

CENTRAL HIGHLANDS

EASTERN

NAIROBI

Scale 1 : 1 000 000
0   10   20   30km

Cross section through Kenya

The cross section below runs through Kenya from the Ugandan border to Mombasa on the Indian Ocean coast. The whole of the area of the Central Highlands is over 1000m above sea level and high plateaux dominate the landscape. The section through Coast Region lies below 500m and consists of a series of low plateaux which run parallel to the coast.

A
Nyeri
Mombasa
B

UGANDA | KENYA
Height in metres
2000
River Turkwel
River Kerio
River Suguta
Central Highlands
Nyeri
River Thika
Coast Region
1000
River Galana
River Voi
Mombasa
500
200
INDIAN OCEAN
A
B

Modified Polyconic projection

Population comparisons

The population of Central Highlands is almost twice that of Coast Region. Both regions have more than doubled their population since 1960.

Central
Coast

Population in millions

4.0
3.5
3.0
2.5
2.0
1.5
1.0
0.5
0

1960 1970 1980 1991 1999

Key

2000 – 3000 m
1000 – 2000 m
500 – 1000 m
200 – 500 m
0 – 200 m

2209 ▲ Mountain height (in metres)
～ River
～ Seasonal river
Lake
── International boundary
── Internal boundary
── Road
── Railway
✈ Airport
○ Town or city

NORTH-EASTERN

EASTERN

COAST

Mbalambala
Saka
▲ 476
Tula
Korokora
Hiraman
Bura
Kathua
Galole Galole
Tana
Kakya
Kiunga
Bodhei
Mkokoni
Pate Island
Hindi
Mkunumbi Lamu
Manda Island
Witu Lamu Island
Garsen
Tiva
Kipini
Ungwana Bay

N
W E
S

Scale 1 : 2 500 000
0   25   50   75   100 km

Noulia 1825 ▲
Tsavo
Tsavo
Manyani
Galana
Mambrui
Malindi
Taita Hills ▲ 2149
Voi
Maktau ▲ 2209 Wundanyi
Taveta
Voi
Penda Kula
Mwatate
Maungu
Bamba
Mtondia
Kilifi
Mackinnon Road
Samburu
Kaloleni
Kasigau 1641 ▲
Mariakani
Changamwe
Kinango Nyali
Mombasa
Kwale
Shimba Hills
Tiwi
Mwereni
Gazi
Chale Point
Ramisi
Shimoni

Climate comparisons

Malindi on the east coast of Kenya enjoys temperatures around 30°C all year round. Nyahururu, the highest town in Kenya has temperatures around 20°C all year. For both towns the wettest month is May.

Facts about Coast Region

Landscape
Area: 83 359 sq km
Highest point: Taita Hills 2209 m

Population
Total: 2 487 264
Density: 29 persons per sq km

Settlement
Regional capital: Mombasa
Other major towns: Malindi, Kilifi

Land use
Main crops: Cashew nuts, sugar cane, fruits
Main industries: Manufacturing, oil refining, vehicle assembly, ship repairing

The Africa Guide
www.africaguide.com
Mombasa Online
www.mombasaonline.com

Nyahururu
Height 2360 metres
°C
35
30
25
20
15
10
5
mm
350
300
250
200
150
100
50
0
J F M A M J J A S O N D

Average monthly temperature
Average monthly rainfall

Malindi
Height 21 metres
°C
35
30
25
20
15
10
5
mm
350
300
250
200
150
100
50
0
J F M A M J J A S O N D

Average monthly rainfall

Modified Polyconic projection

Tourism

Tourism makes an important contribution to Kenya's economy. The main attractions are wildlife in the National Parks and National Reserves, and the resorts on the Indian Ocean coast. The temperature is over 20°C throughout the country all year.

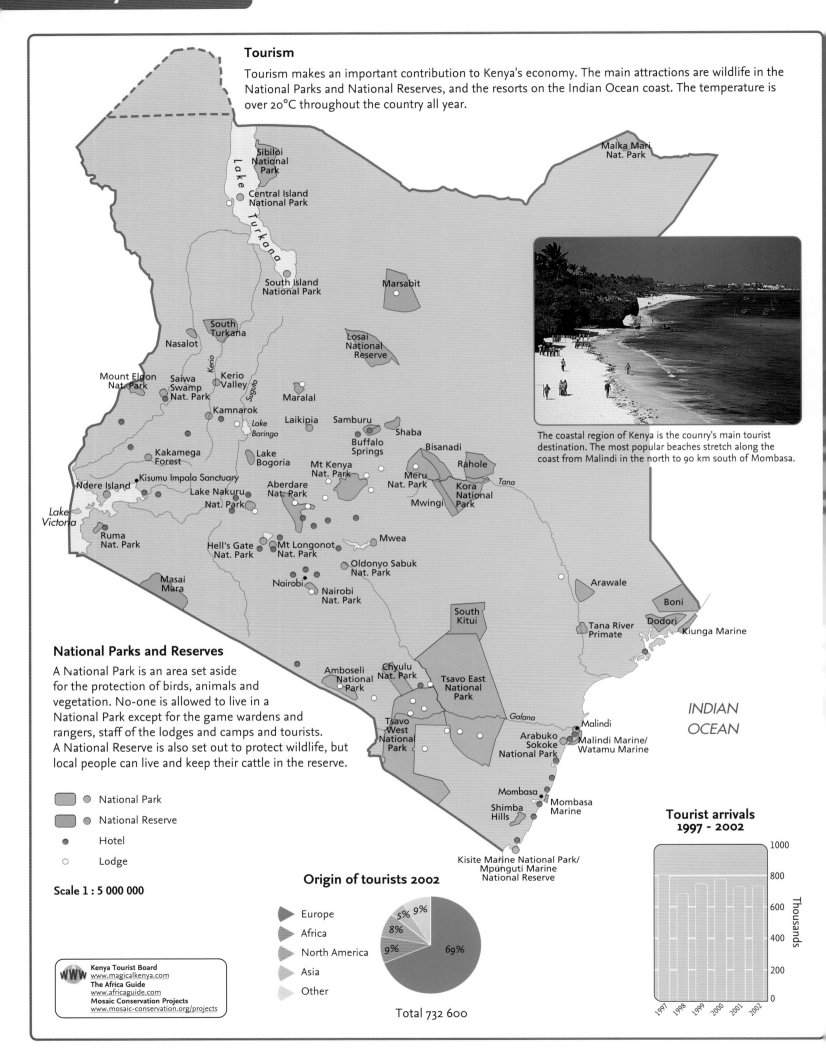

The coastal region of Kenya is the counry's main tourist destination. The most popular beaches stretch along the coast from Malindi in the north to 90 km south of Mombasa.

Malka Mari Nat. Park

Sibiloi National Park

Central Island National Park

Lake Turkana

South Island National Park

Marsabit

South Turkana

Nasalot

Losai National Reserve

Kerio

Mount Elgon Nat. Park

Saiwa Swamp Nat. Park

Kerio Valley

Suguta

Maralal

Kamnarok

Lake Baringo

Laikipia

Samburu

Shaba

Buffalo Springs

Bisanadi

Rahole

Kakamega Forest

Lake Bogoria

Mt Kenya Nat. Park

Meru Nat. Park

Kora National Park

Tana

Ndere Island

Kisumu Impala Sanctuary

Lake Nakuru Nat. Park

Aberdare Nat. Park

Mwingi

Lake Victoria

Ruma Nat. Park

Hell's Gate Nat. Park

Mt Longonot Nat. Park

Mwea

Oldonyo Sabuk Nat. Park

Masai Mara

Nairobi

Nairobi Nat. Park

Arawale

Boni

South Kitui

Tana River Primate

Dodori

Kiunga Marine

National Parks and Reserves

A National Park is an area set aside for the protection of birds, animals and vegetation. No-one is allowed to live in a National Park except for the game wardens and rangers, staff of the lodges and camps and tourists. A National Reserve is also set out to protect wildlife, but local people can live and keep their cattle in the reserve.

Amboseli National Park

Chyulu Nat. Park

Tsavo East National Park

Galana

Malindi

INDIAN OCEAN

Tsavo West National Park

Arabuko Sokoke National Park

Malindi Marine/ Watamu Marine

Mombasa

Mombasa Marine

Shimba Hills

	National Park
	National Reserve
•	Hotel
○	Lodge

Scale 1 : 5 000 000

Kisite Marine National Park/ Mpunguti Marine National Reserve

Kenya Tourist Board
www.magicalkenya.com
The Africa Guide
www.africaguide.com
Mosaic Conservation Projects
www.mosaic-conservation.org/projects

Origin of tourists 2002

- ▶ Europe
- ▶ Africa
- ▶ North America
- ▷ Asia
- ▷ Other

5% 9%
8%
9% 69%

Total 732 600

Tourist arrivals 1997 - 2002

Thousands

1000
800
600
400
200
0

1997 1998 1999 2000 2001 2002

Masai Mara National Reserve

Situated on the border with Tanzania, the Masai Mara National Reserve is one of Kenya's best known wildlife reserves. Animals such as gazelles, elephants, cheetahs, buffalo and a few black rhino live here all year round. During July and October over one million wildebeest and a quarter of a million zebra move through the Masai Mara on their migrations from and to the Serengeti in Tanzania.

Game Reserve.com
www.game-reserve.com

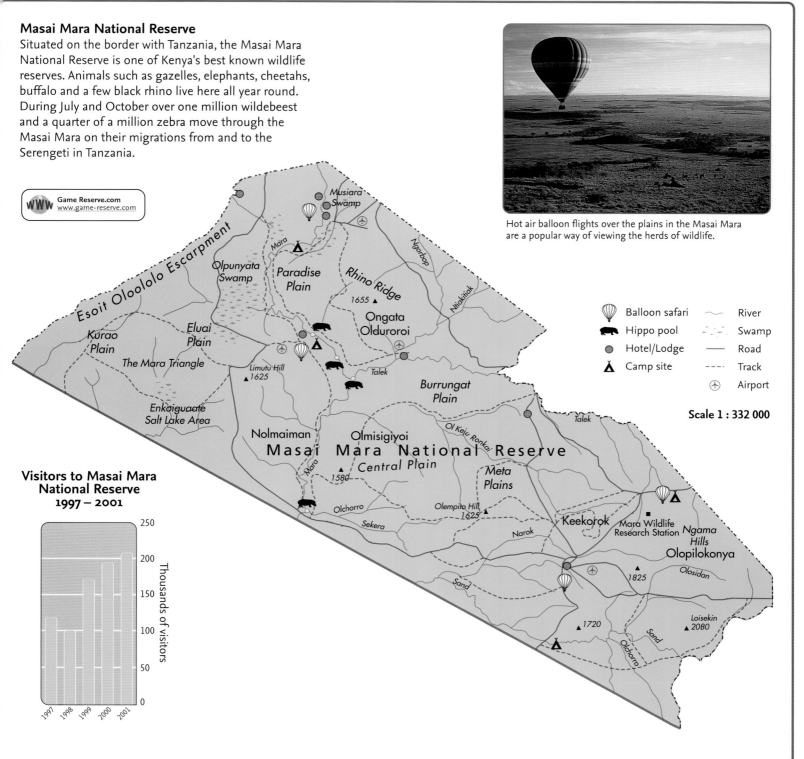

Hot air balloon flights over the plains in the Masai Mara are a popular way of viewing the herds of wildlife.

Symbol	Feature	Symbol	Feature
Balloon safari		River	
Hippo pool		Swamp	
Hotel/Lodge		Road	
Camp site		Track	
		Airport	

Scale 1 : 332 000

Visitors to Masai Mara National Reserve 1997 – 2001

Thousands of visitors

250
200
150
100
50
0

1997 1998 1999 2000 2001

Africa's top tourist destinations 2002

Rank	Country	Visitors
1	South Africa	6 550 000
2	Tunisia	5 506 000
3	Egypt	4 906 000
4	Morocco	4 193 000
5	Botswana	1 037 000
6	Algeria	998 000
7	Kenya	838 000
8	Mauritius	682 000
9	Zambia	565 000
10	Tanzania	550 000
11	Ghana	483 000

For four months every year herds of wildebeest from Tanzania graze on the Mara plains. Tall grasses are reduced to stubble before the herds trek south again.

Hippos can be found wallowing in pools in the Mara river.

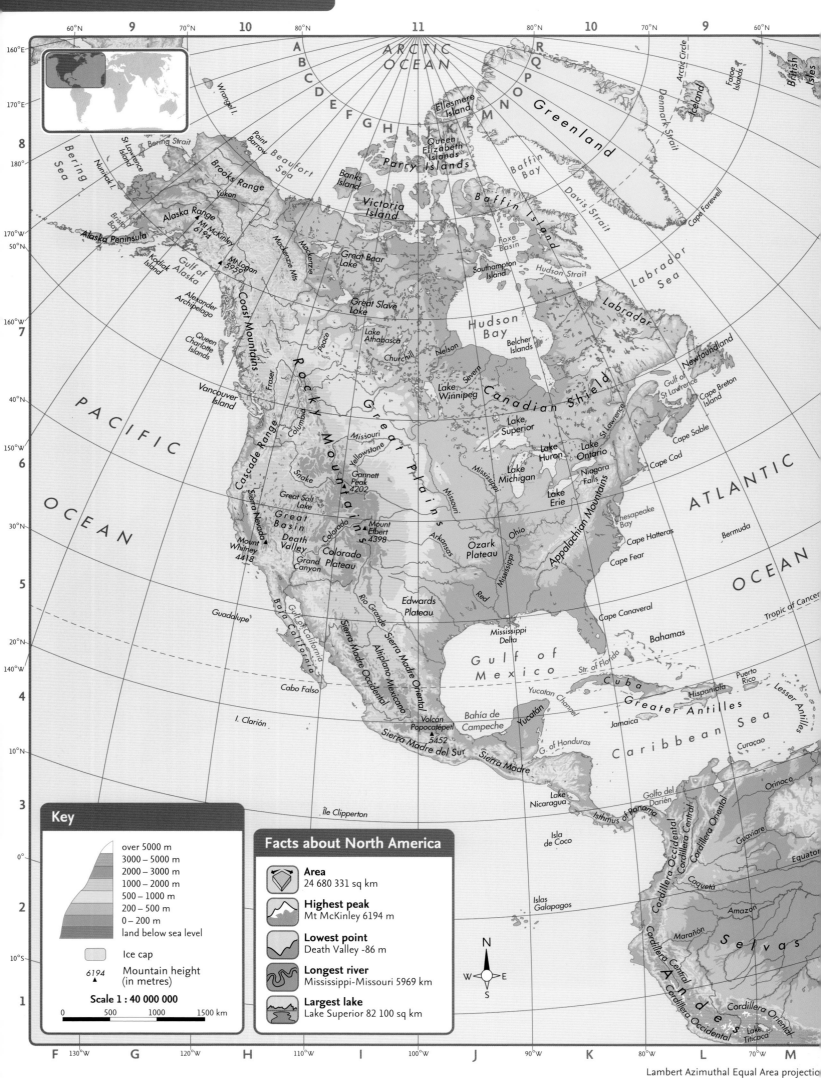

ARCTIC OCEAN

Wrangel I.

Point Barrow

Beaufort Sea

Brooks Range

Yukon

Alaska Range
Mt McKinley 6194

Mt Logan 5959

Alaska Peninsula

Kodiak Island

Gulf of Alaska

Alexander Archipelago

Queen Charlotte Islands

Coast Mountains

Vancouver Island

St Lawrence Island

Nunivak I.

Bering Strait

Bering Sea

Bristol Bay

Mackenzie Mts

Mackenzie

Great Bear Lake

Great Slave Lake

Lake Athabasca

Peace

Churchill

Nelson

Severn

Banks Island

Victoria Island

Parry Islands

Queen Elizabeth Islands

Ellesmere Island

Foxe Basin

Southampton Island

Hudson Strait

Hudson Bay

Belcher Islands

Baffin Island

Baffin Bay

Davis Strait

Greenland

Denmark Strait

Cape Farewell

Arctic Circle

Iceland

Faroe Islands

British Isles

Labrador Sea

Labrador

Newfoundland

Gulf of St Lawrence

Cape Breton Island

Cape Sable

Canadian Shield

Lake Winnipeg

Lake Superior

Lake Huron

Lake Michigan

Lake Ontario

Lake Erie

Niagara Falls

Appalachian Mountains

Chesapeake Bay

Cape Cod

Cape Hatteras

Cape Fear

Cape Canaveral

Bermuda

ATLANTIC OCEAN

PACIFIC OCEAN

Rocky Mountains

Great Plains

Cascade Range

Columbia

Snake

Fraser

Sierra Nevada

Great Salt Lake

Great Basin

Death Valley

Mount Whitney 4418

Colorado

Grand Canyon

Colorado Plateau

Gannett Peak 4202

Yellowstone

Missouri

Mount Elbert 4398

Arkansas

Red

Mississippi

Missouri

Ohio

Ozark Plateau

Edwards Plateau

Rio Grande

Guadalupe

Cabo Falso

I. Clarión

Île Clipperton

Baja California

Gulf of California

Sierra Madre Occidental

Altiplano Mexicano

Sierra Madre Oriental

Sierra Madre del Sur

Volcán Popocatépetl 5452

Bahía de Campeche

Yucatán

Yucatan Channel

Mississippi Delta

Gulf of Mexico

Str. of Florida

Cuba

Bahamas

Greater Antilles

Hispaniola

Puerto Rico

Lesser Antilles

Jamaica

Caribbean Sea

Curaçao

G. of Honduras

Lake Nicaragua

Golfo del Darién

Isthmus of Panamá

Isla de Coco

Islas Galápagos

Sierra Madre

Tropic of Cancer

Orinoco

Guaviare

Equator

Caquetá

Marañón

Amazon

Selvas

Andes

Cordillera Occidental

Cordillera Central

Cordillera Oriental

Cordillera Central

Cordillera Occidental

Cordillera Oriental

Lake Titicaca

Key

- over 5000 m
- 3000 – 5000 m
- 2000 – 3000 m
- 1000 – 2000 m
- 500 – 1000 m
- 200 – 500 m
- 0 – 200 m
- land below sea level

Ice cap

6194 ▲ Mountain height (in metres)

Scale 1 : 40 000 000

0   500   1000   1500 km

Facts about North America

Area
24 680 331 sq km

Highest peak
Mt McKinley 6194 m

Lowest point
Death Valley -86 m

Longest river
Mississippi-Missouri 5969 km

Largest lake
Lake Superior 82 100 sq km

N
W   E
S

Lambert Azimuthal Equal Area projection

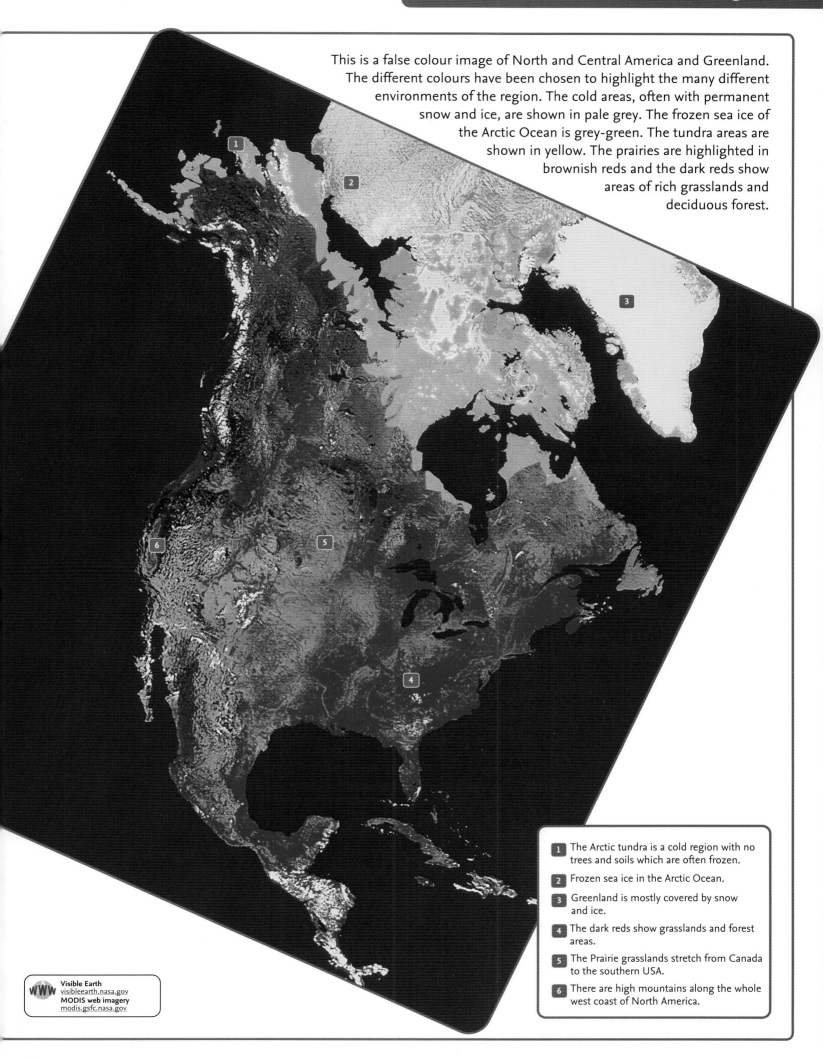

This is a false colour image of North and Central America and Greenland. The different colours have been chosen to highlight the many different environments of the region. The cold areas, often with permanent snow and ice, are shown in pale grey. The frozen sea ice of the Arctic Ocean is grey-green. The tundra areas are shown in yellow. The prairies are highlighted in brownish reds and the dark reds show areas of rich grasslands and deciduous forest.

1 The Arctic tundra is a cold region with no trees and soils which are often frozen.

2 Frozen sea ice in the Arctic Ocean.

3 Greenland is mostly covered by snow and ice.

4 The dark reds show grasslands and forest areas.

5 The Prairie grasslands stretch from Canada to the southern USA.

6 There are high mountains along the whole west coast of North America.

Visible Earth
visibleearth.nasa.gov
MODIS web imagery
modis.gsfc.nasa.gov

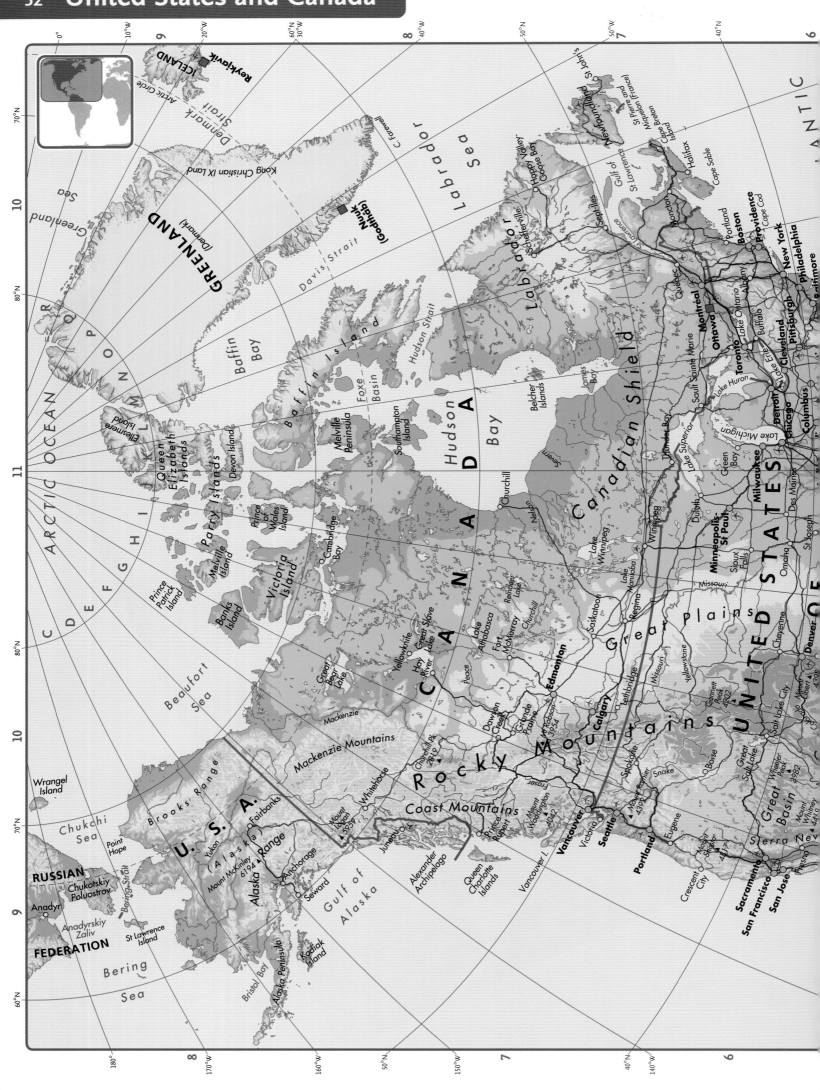

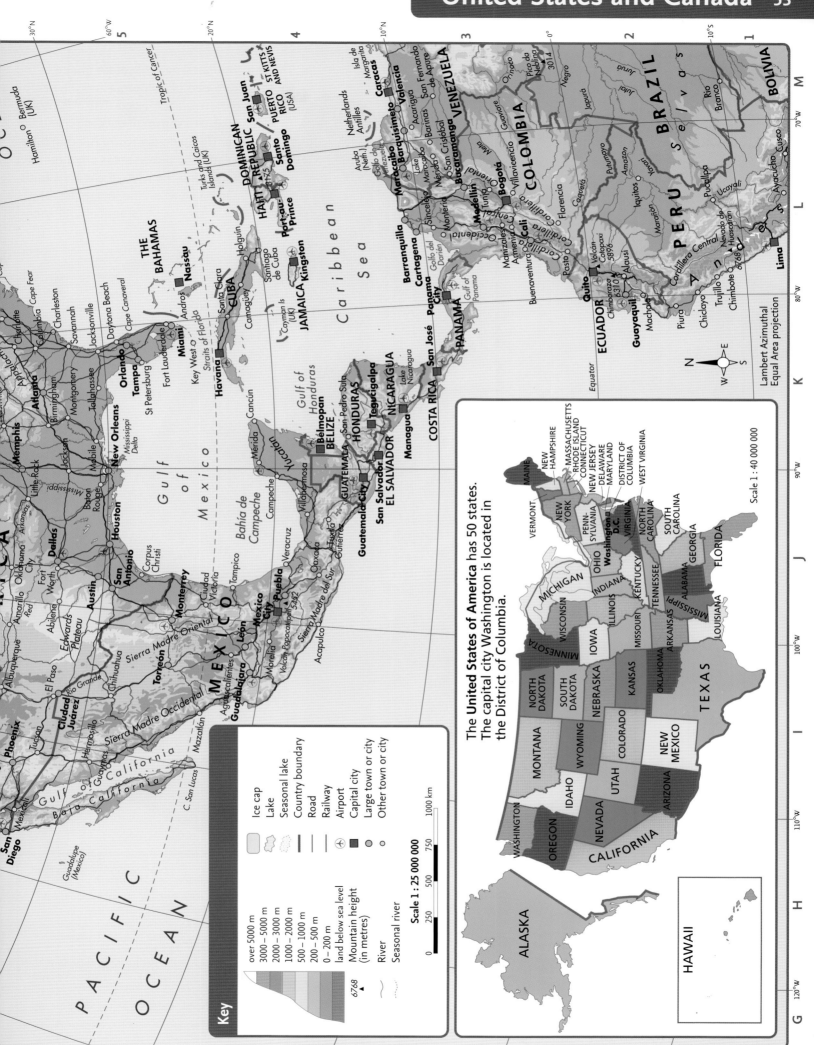

Key

	Ice cap
	Lake
	Seasonal lake
	Country boundary
	Road
	Railway
✈	Airport
■	Capital city
●	Large town or city
○	Other town or city

Scale 1 : 25 000 000

0   250   500   750   1000 km

over 5000 m
3000 – 5000 m
2000 – 3000 m
1000 – 2000 m
500 – 1000 m
200 – 500 m
0 – 200 m
land below sea level

Mountain height
(in metres)

6768 ▲

River
Seasonal river

The United States of America has 50 states. The capital city Washington is located in the District of Columbia.

Scale 1 : 40 000 000

This is a simulated natural colour image of the southwestern part of California and the nearby area of northwest Mexico. The oceans and large lakes are shown in dark blue, and the river Colorado is shown as a thin blue-black line. The brown areas are mountain ranges and the white areas are clouds. Green areas on the image are forests or agricultural zones.

WWW **Visible Earth**
visibleearth.nasa.gov
MODIS web imagery
modis.gsfc.nasa.gov

1 Lake Powell provides water for irrigation and tourism in the desert.

2 Lake Mead has formed behind the Hoover Dam.

3 Los Angeles has grown so large it has to bring in water from all the rivers of southern California.

4 So much water has been taken from the river Colorado that only a trickle reaches the Gulf of California.

5 Forest vegetation on the Sierra Madre.

This is a natural colour image showing Hurricane Isabel in the Caribbean Sea on 15th September 2003. The hurricane, an enormous rotating storm, appears clearly as a white swirl of cloud. Winds are strongest in the centre of the swirl where they reached 160 kph. The green areas are land and the blue-green areas are the shallow waters around The Bahamas. Hurricane Isabel hit land on the US east coast on 17th September 2003.

1	The eye or centre of the hurricane.
2	The Bahamas
3	Cuba
4	Haiti
5	Dominican Republic

WWW National Hurricane Center
www.nhc.noaa.gov
National Oceanic and Atmospheric Administration
www.noaa.gov

Hurricane tracks
Hurricanes originate in the warm, moist tropical air over the Atlantic Ocean and move westwards at about 20 kph. Their power declines rapidly as they pass over land or cooler water and they usually last for about 9 days.

Hurricane risk

Scale 1: 50 000 000

Chance of a hurricane during one year

| less than 5% | 5 – 35% | 35 – 55% | 55 – 65% | 65 – 90% |

Scale 1: 50 000 000

Tracks of major hurricanes 1980-2004

→ Allen 1980	→ Gordon 1994	→ Floyd 1999
→ Gilbert 1988	→ Fran 1996	→ Isabel 2003
→ Andrew 1992	→ Mitch 1998	→ Charley 2004

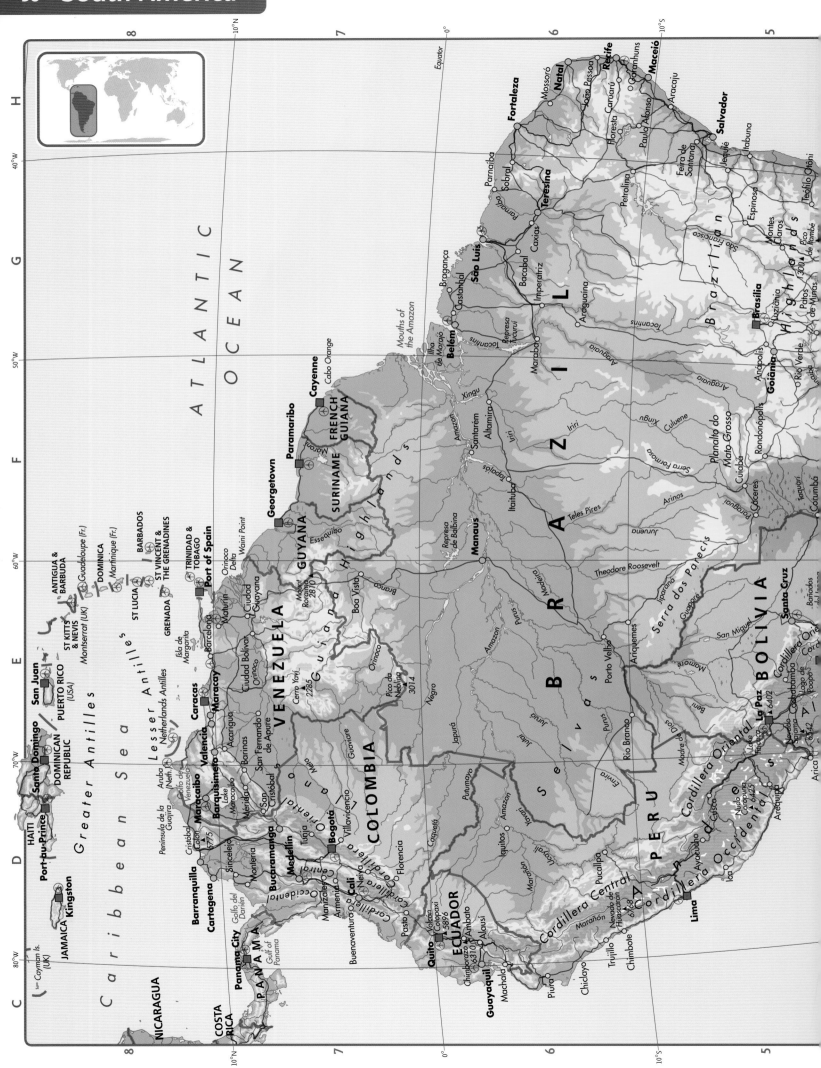

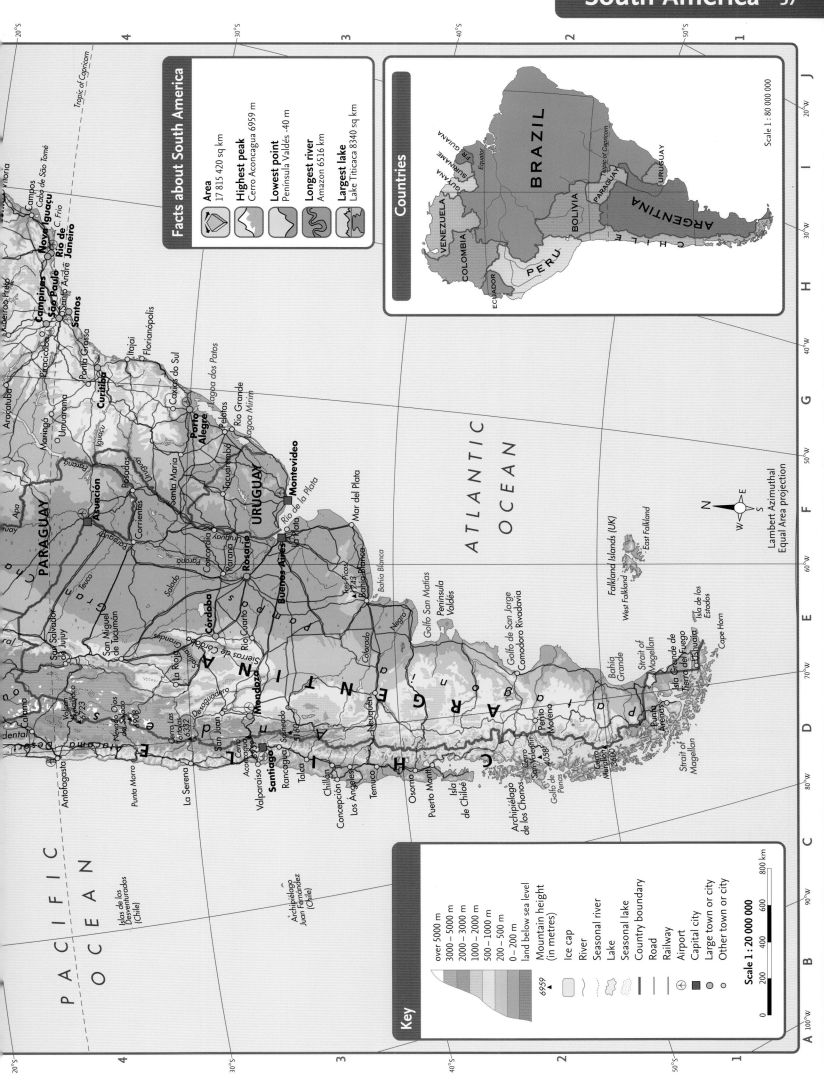

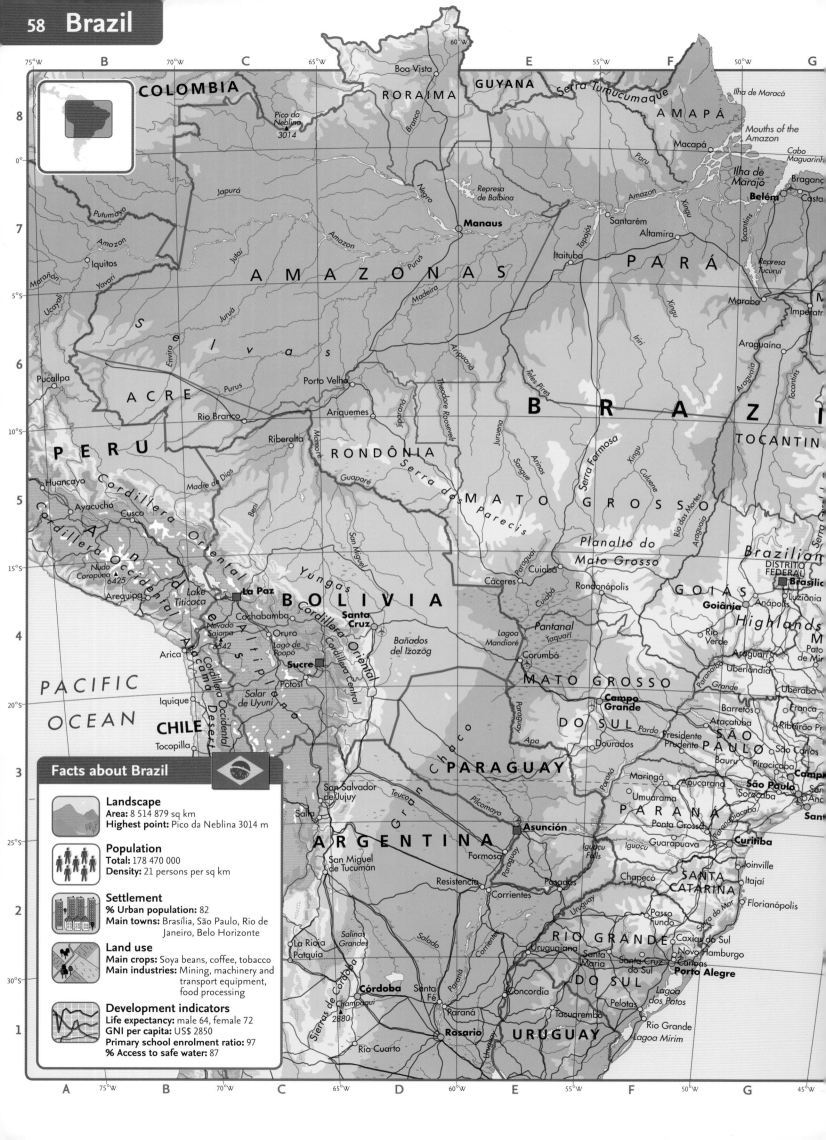

Facts about Brazil

Landscape
Area: 8 514 879 sq km
Highest point: Pico da Neblina 3014 m

Population
Total: 178 470 000
Density: 21 persons per sq km

Settlement
% Urban population: 82
Main towns: Brasília, São Paulo, Rio de Janeiro, Belo Horizonte

Land use
Main crops: Soya beans, coffee, tobacco
Main industries: Mining, machinery and transport equipment, food processing

Development indicators
Life expectancy: male 64, female 72
GNI per capita: US$ 2850
Primary school enrolment ratio: 97
% Access to safe water: 87

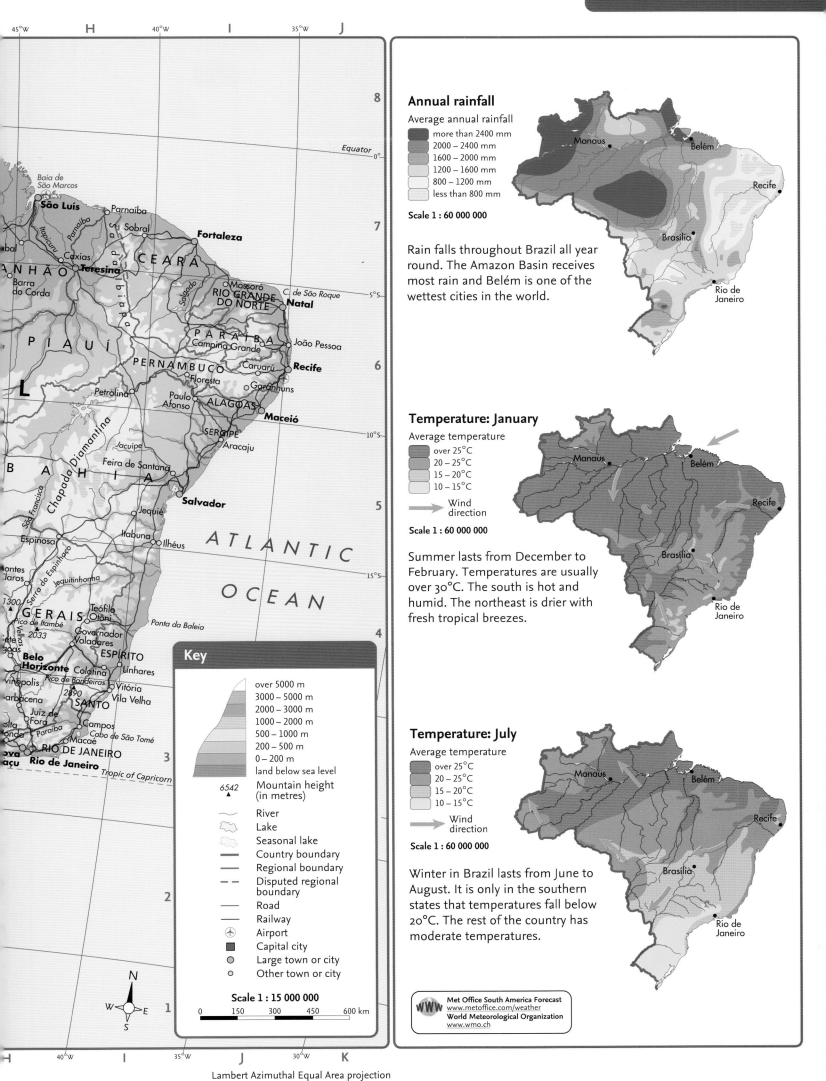

Map labels (main map)

Baía de São Marcos
São Luís
Parnaíba
Sobral
Fortaleza
Caxias
Teresina
CEARÁ
ANHÃO
Barra do Corda
Itapicuru
Parnaíba
Mossoró
RIO GRANDE DO NORTE
Salgado
C. de São Roque
Natal
PIAUÍ
PARAÍBA
Campina Grande
João Pessoa
PERNAMBUCO
Caruaru
Recife
L
Floresta
Garanhuns
Petrolina
Paulo Afonso
ALAGOAS
SERGIPE
Maceió
Aracaju
BAHIA
Jacuípe
Feira de Santana
Chapada Diamantina
São Francisco
Espinosa
Jequié
Itabuna
Ilhéus
ATLANTIC OCEAN
Jequitinhonha
Serra do Espinhaço
Montes Claros
1300
GERAIS
Teófilo Otóni
Pico de Itambé 2033
velhas
gas
Governador Valadares
ESPÍRITO
Linhares
Belo Horizonte
Colatina
inópolis
Pico de Bandeiras 2890
Vitória
SANTO
Vila Velha
arbacena
Juiz de Fora
Campos
Cabo de São Tomé
olta
Paraíba
Macaé
RIO DE JANEIRO
ova
onda
açu
Rio de Janeiro
Tropic of Capricorn
Ponta da Baleia

Equator 0°
5°S
10°S
15°S

Key

over 5000 m
3000 – 5000 m
2000 – 3000 m
1000 – 2000 m
500 – 1000 m
200 – 500 m
0 – 200 m
land below sea level

6542 ▲ Mountain height (in metres)

River
Lake
Seasonal lake
Country boundary
Regional boundary
Disputed regional boundary
Road
Railway
✈ Airport
■ Capital city
◉ Large town or city
◦ Other town or city

Scale 1 : 15 000 000

0 150 300 450 600 km

N
W E
S

Lambert Azimuthal Equal Area projection

Annual rainfall

Average annual rainfall

- more than 2400 mm
- 2000 – 2400 mm
- 1600 – 2000 mm
- 1200 – 1600 mm
- 800 – 1200 mm
- less than 800 mm

Scale 1 : 60 000 000

Rain falls throughout Brazil all year round. The Amazon Basin receives most rain and Belém is one of the wettest cities in the world.

Manaus · Belém · Recife · Brasília · Rio de Janeiro

Temperature: January

Average temperature

- over 25°C
- 20 – 25°C
- 15 – 20°C
- 10 – 15°C

→ Wind direction

Scale 1 : 60 000 000

Summer lasts from December to February. Temperatures are usually over 30°C. The south is hot and humid. The northeast is drier with fresh tropical breezes.

Manaus · Belém · Recife · Brasília · Rio de Janeiro

Temperature: July

Average temperature

- over 25°C
- 20 – 25°C
- 15 – 20°C
- 10 – 15°C

→ Wind direction

Scale 1 : 60 000 000

Winter in Brazil lasts from June to August. It is only in the southern states that temperatures fall below 20°C. The rest of the country has moderate temperatures.

Manaus · Belém · Recife · Brasília · Rio de Janeiro

WWW Met Office South America Forecast
www.metoffice.com/weather
World Meteorological Organization
www.wmo.ch

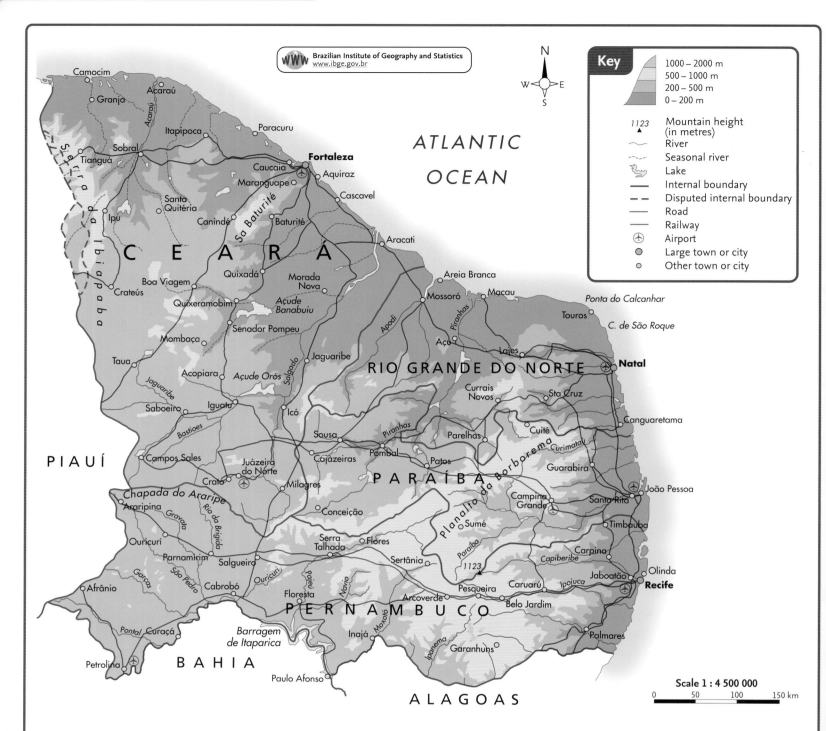

Brazilian Institute of Geography and Statistics
www.ibge.gov.br

Key

1000 – 2000 m
500 – 1000 m
200 – 500 m
0 – 200 m

1123 ▲ Mountain height (in metres)
River
Seasonal river
Lake
Internal boundary
Disputed internal boundary
Road
Railway
⊕ Airport
● Large town or city
○ Other town or city

ATLANTIC OCEAN

Scale 1 : 4 500 000

0   50   100   150 km

Population

Since the 1960's the growth of population has been constant. Most of the population live on or near the coast.

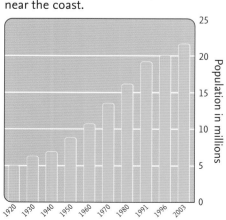

Population in millions

1920 1930 1940 1950 1960 1970 1980 1991 1996 2003

Employment

Northeast Brazil provides few employment opportunities in the manufacturing sector. Just over a third of the workforce make a living from agriculture.

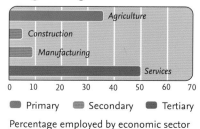

Agriculture
Construction
Manufacturing
Services

0 10 20 30 40 50 60 70

■ Primary ■ Secondary ■ Tertiary

Percentage employed by economic sector

Facts about Northeast Coast

Landscape
Area: 356 375 sq km
Highest point: 1123 m

Population
Total: 21 569 612
Density: 60 persons per sq km

Settlement
% Urban population: 74
Main towns/cities: Recife, Fortaleza, Natal

Land use
Main crops: Haricot beans, maize, sugar cane, cashew nuts
Main industries: Engineering, chemicals, textiles, food processing

Lambert Azimuthal Equal Area projection

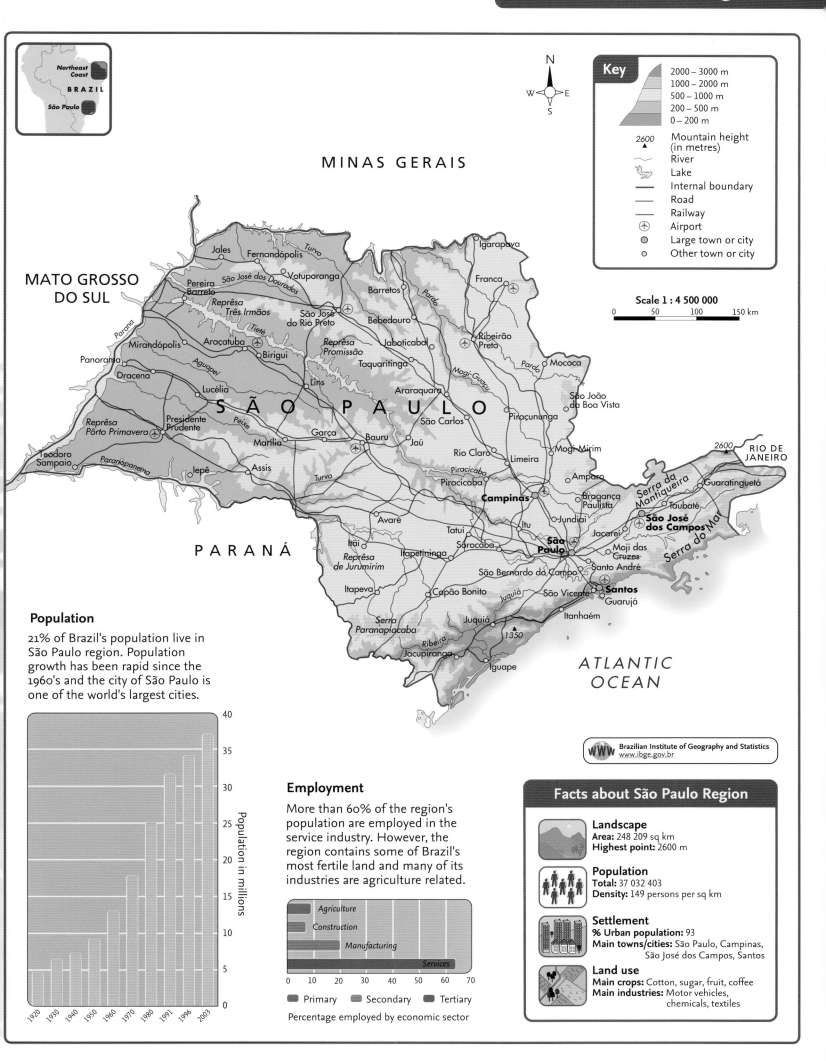

Northeast Coast
BRAZIL
São Paulo

Key

	2000 – 3000 m
	1000 – 2000 m
	500 – 1000 m
	200 – 500 m
	0 – 200 m

2600 ▲ Mountain height (in metres)
River
Lake
Internal boundary
Road
Railway
✈ Airport
◉ Large town or city
○ Other town or city

Scale 1 : 4 500 000
0   50   100   150 km

MINAS GERAIS

MATO GROSSO DO SUL

S Ã O   P A U L O

PARANÁ

RIO DE JANEIRO

ATLANTIC OCEAN

Map labels
Jales, Fernandópolis, Turvo, Igarapava, Pereira Barreto, Votuporanga, São José dos Dourados, Franca, Barretos, Represa Três Irmãos, São José do Rio Preto, Bebedouro, Pardo, Tietê, Jaboticabal, Ribeirão Preto, Araçatuba, Birigui, Represa Promissão, Taquaritinga, Mococa, Pardo, Mirandópolis, Aguapeí, Lins, Mogi-Guaçu, São João da Boa Vista, Panorama, Dracena, Lucélia, Araraquara, São Carlos, Piraçununga, Parana, Peixe, Garça, Bauru, Jaú, Rio Claro, Limeira, Mogi-Mirim, Represa Pôrto Primavera, Presidente Prudente, Marília, Amparo, 2600, Teodoro Sampaio, Paranapanema, Iepê, Assis, Turvo, Piracicaba, Bragança Paulista, Guaratinguetá, Avaré, Piracicaba, Campinas, Serra da Mantiqueira, Taubaté, Tatuí, Itu, Jundiaí, São José dos Campos, Itaí, Sorocaba, Jacareí, Serra do Mar, Represa de Jurumirim, Itapetininga, São Paulo, Moji das Cruzes, Itapeva, Capão Bonito, São Bernardo do Campo, Santo André, Juquiá, São Vicente, Santos, Guarujá, Serra Paranapiacaba, Juquiá, Itanhaém, Ribeira, 1350, Jacupiranga, Iguape

Population

21% of Brazil's population live in São Paulo region. Population growth has been rapid since the 1960's and the city of São Paulo is one of the world's largest cities.

Population in millions
40, 35, 30, 25, 20, 15, 10, 5, 0
1920, 1930, 1940, 1950, 1960, 1970, 1980, 1991, 1996, 2003

Employment

More than 60% of the region's population are employed in the service industry. However, the region contains some of Brazil's most fertile land and many of its industries are agriculture related.

Agriculture
Construction
Manufacturing
Services

0   10   20   30   40   50   60   70

■ Primary   ■ Secondary   ■ Tertiary
Percentage employed by economic sector

Facts about São Paulo Region

Landscape
Area: 248 209 sq km
Highest point: 2600 m

Population
Total: 37 032 403
Density: 149 persons per sq km

Settlement
% Urban population: 93
Main towns/cities: São Paulo, Campinas, São José dos Campos, Santos

Land use
Main crops: Cotton, sugar, fruit, coffee
Main industries: Motor vehicles, chemicals, textiles

Lambert Azimuthal Equal Area projection

This is a false colour image of part of the Amazon rainforest. The river Jiparana is a tributary of the Amazon and flows across the image as a black line from left to right. The straight lines in the forest show where whole blocks of trees have been cut down. This image shows the link between weather conditions and the forest as the orange area in the south of the image is a rainstorm.

1 The green and blue areas are used for farming.

2 The pink areas are where the rainforest has not yet been cut down.

3 River Jiparana

Amazonia : Development

The largest tropical rainforest in the world is in Amazonia in Brazil. Most deforestation has taken place on the edges of the forest in the east, south and southwest. Satellite images like the one opposite allow the Brazilian government to monitor damage to the forest and take steps to prevent unnecessary exploitation of the forest.

■ Location of satellite image shown on page 62

HEP developments
— HEP Dam
— HEP Dam (planned)

Communications
—— Railway
----- Railway (planned)
—— Road
----- Road (planned)

Land Use
☐ Cropland and woodland
☐ Grassland and grazing
☐ Grassland and woodland
☐ Tropical forest
☐ Temperate forest
☐ Scrubland or desert
☐ Swamp or marsh
☐ Deforestation
—— Extent of Amazonia in Brazil

Scale 1 : 30 000 000

Brazil : Resources

Brazil has a wide variety of mineral resources. It produces high grade manganese and iron ore which are its main exports. Industry is concentrated around the main cities where over 75% of the population live.

Minerals and fuel
■ Iron ore
■ Tin
● Manganese
✕ Bauxite
● Gold
◆ Diamonds
▲ Lead and Zinc
◆ Copper
■ Chromium
◆ Nickel
⬬ Coalfield
⬬ Oilfield and oilsand
⬬ Gasfield
—— Oil pipeline
—— Gas pipeline

Industry
▱ Iron / Steel
▥ Oil refineries
▣ Shipbuilding
✈ Aircraft
✵ Mechanical engineering
▯ Electronics
▨ Publishing / Paper
▧ Chemicals
▤ Textiles / Clothing
▣ Food processing
• Major industrial centre

Scale 1 : 30 000 000

www Brazilian Institute of Geography and Statistics
www.ibge.gov.br

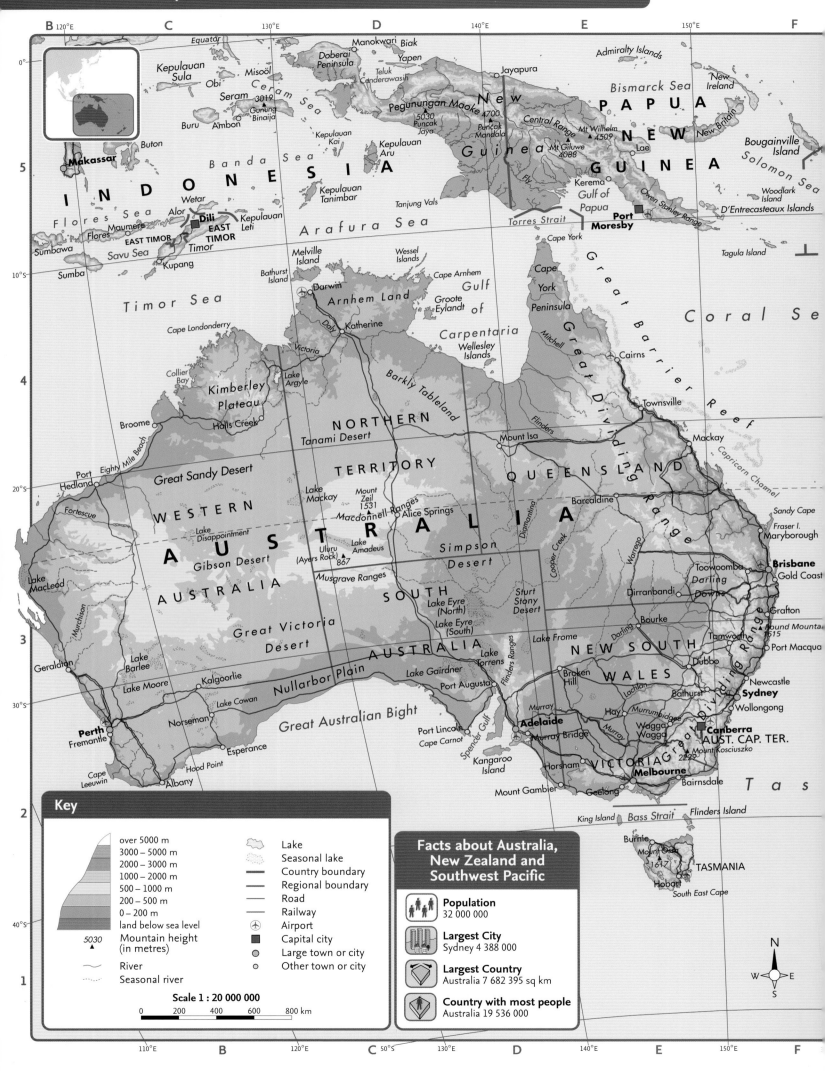

Key

over 5000 m	
3000 – 5000 m	
2000 – 3000 m	
1000 – 2000 m	
500 – 1000 m	
200 – 500 m	
0 – 200 m	
land below sea level	

5030   ▲ Mountain height (in metres)

~~~~~ River

········· Seasonal river

Lake

Seasonal lake

——— Country boundary

——— Regional boundary

——— Road

——— Railway

✈ Airport

■ Capital city

⬤ Large town or city

○ Other town or city

Scale 1 : 20 000 000

0   200   400   600   800 km

Facts about Australia, New Zealand and Southwest Pacific

Population
32 000 000

Largest City
Sydney 4 388 000

Largest Country
Australia 7 682 395 sq km

Country with most people
Australia 19 536 000

N
W · E
S

160°E　　G　　170°E　　H

Kingsmill Group

NAURU

KIRIBATI

5

...seul

Santa Isabel

SOLOMON

ISLANDS

TUVALU

Nui　　Vaitupu

Nukufetau

Funafuti ✈

Vaiaku

Malaita

...niara

...dalcanal

San Cristobal

Santa Cruz
Islands

Rennell

10°S

Banks Islands

VANUATU

Espíritu Santo

Malakula

Éfaté ✈ **Port Vila**

Erromango

Vanua Levu

FIJI

Viti Levu ✈
Suva

Kadavu

4

Îles
Loyauté

20°S

New Caledonia
(France)

✈
Nouméa

Tropic of Capricorn

P A C I F I C   O C E A N

Norfolk Island
(Australia)

3

30°S

Lord Howe Island
(Australia)

...n　　S e a

Cape Maria van Diemen　　North Cape

North Island

2

Auckland

Manukau

Hamilton

Bay of
Plenty

East Cape

Mount Taranaki
(Mount Egmont)　▲2518

NEW

Cape Farewell　Palmerston
North

Napier

ZEALAND

Nelson

✈**Wellington**

40°S

Aoraki
(Mount Cook)

3754 ▲

Southern Alps

Cook Strait

Chatham Islands
(New Zealand)

South Island

Christchurch

Cape Providence

Lake
Te Anau

1

Stewart Island

Dunedin

Bounty Islands
(New Zealand)

Antipodes Islands
(New Zealand)

Auckland Islands
(New Zealand)

G　　170°E　　H　　180°　　50°S　　I　　170°W

Lambert Azimuthal Equal Area projection

Bushfires

In Australia bushfires are a serious hazard in the dry season especially in the southeast and southwest of the continent.

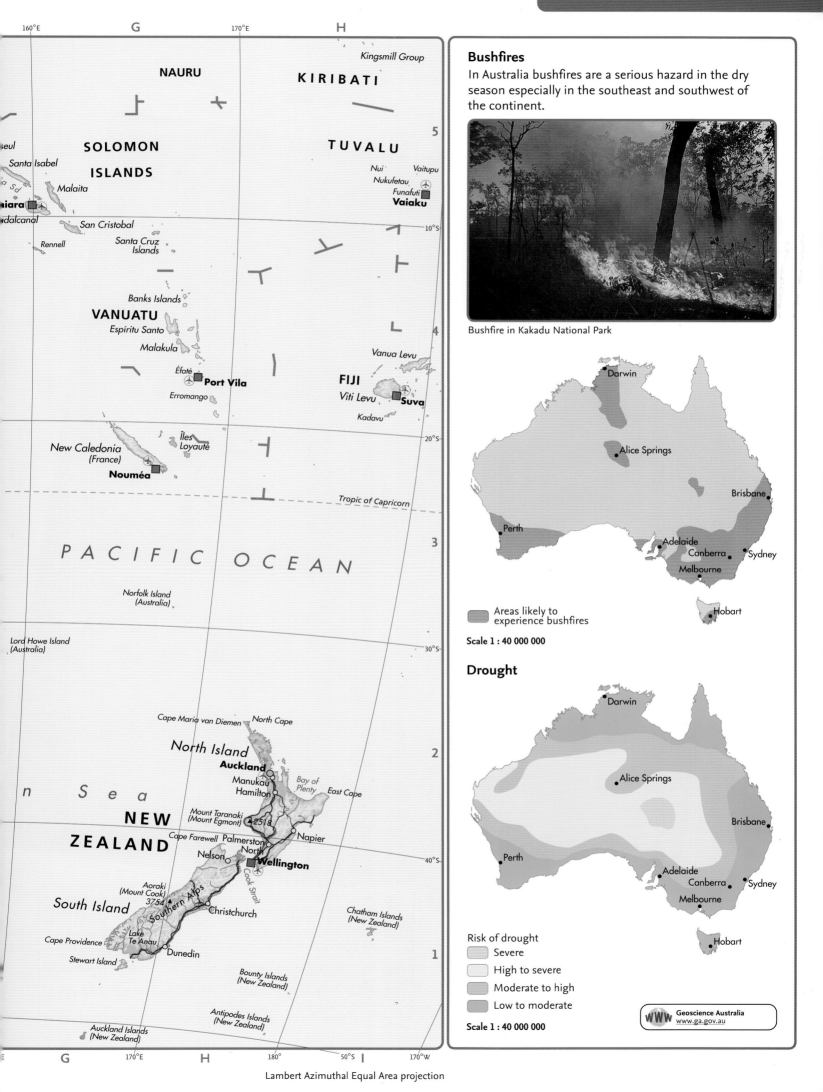

Bushfire in Kakadu National Park

Darwin

Alice Springs

Brisbane

Perth

Adelaide
Canberra
Sydney

Melbourne

Hobart

▨ Areas likely to experience bushfires

Scale 1 : 40 000 000

Drought

Darwin

Alice Springs

Brisbane

Perth

Adelaide
Canberra
Sydney

Melbourne

Hobart

Risk of drought
▨ Severe
▨ High to severe
▨ Moderate to high
▨ Low to moderate

Scale 1 : 40 000 000

WWW Geoscience Australia
www.ga.gov.au

This is a simulated natural colour image of Australia, New Zealand and the nearby parts of southeast Asia and the southwest Pacific Ocean. The desert of central and western Australia is shown in pink-brown, whilst the greens on the image show those areas with forests and farmland. Areas of grassland are shown in grey-green.

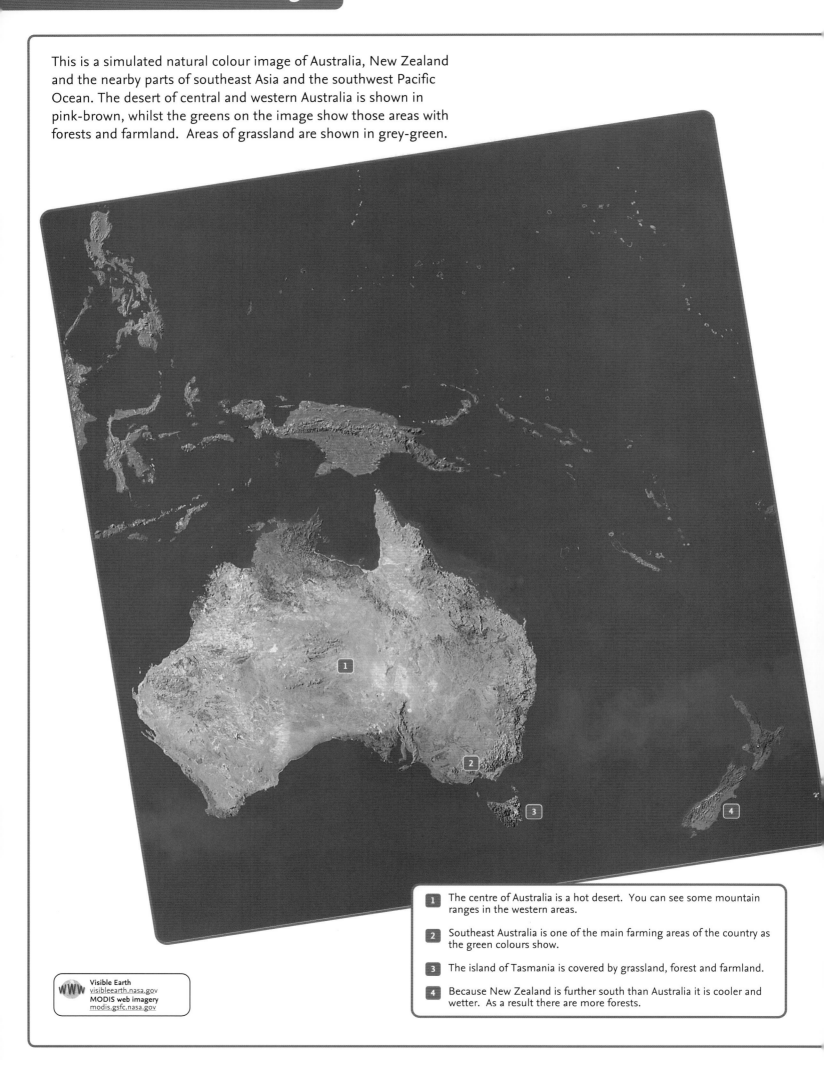

1 The centre of Australia is a hot desert. You can see some mountain ranges in the western areas.

2 Southeast Australia is one of the main farming areas of the country as the green colours show.

3 The island of Tasmania is covered by grassland, forest and farmland.

4 Because New Zealand is further south than Australia it is cooler and wetter. As a result there are more forests.

Annual rainfall

Average annual rainfall

- 1000 – 2000 mm
- 500 – 1000 mm
- 250 – 500 mm
- less than 250 mm

Scale 1 : 60 000 000

Australia is the driest continent and rainfall is highly variable across the country. The wettest areas are northeast Queensland and southwest Tasmania; the centre of Australia is hot and dry.

Population

Persons per sq km

- over 50
- 10 – 50
- 1 – 10
- 0 – 1

Cities and towns

- ● 2 500 000 – 5 000 000
- • 1 000 000 – 2 500 000

Scale 1 : 60 000 000

Brisbane
Perth
Adelaide
Sydney
Melbourne

Australia has one of the lowest population densities in the world. Distribution is uneven with most people living along the eastern and south eastern coasts. The main urban areas are Adelaide, Brisbane, Melbourne, Perth and Sydney.

Temperature: January

Average temperature

- over 32°C
- 24 – 32°C
- 16 – 24°C
- 8 – 16°C

→ Wind direction

Scale 1 : 60 000 000

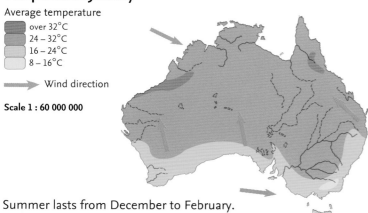

Summer lasts from December to February. In January average temperatures exceed 3°C. The hottest areas are northwest Western Australia and from southwest Queensland across south Australia into southeast Western Australia.

WWW
World Meteorological Organization
www.wmo.ch
Met Office Australasia Forecast
www.metoffice.com/weather
Australian Bureau of Statistics
www.abs.gov.au

Sydney

Space Imaging

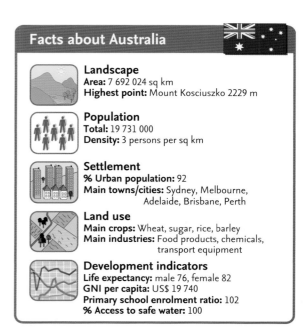

Sydney is Australia's largest city with a population of 4 388 000.

Temperature: July

Average temperature

- over 24°C
- 16 – 24°C
- 8 – 16°C
- 0 – 8°C
- below 0°C

→ Wind direction

Scale 1 : 60 000 000

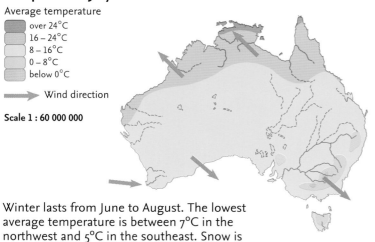

Winter lasts from June to August. The lowest average temperature is between 7°C in the northwest and 5°C in the southeast. Snow is confined to the mountainous regions of the southeast.

Facts about Australia

Landscape
Area: 7 692 024 sq km
Highest point: Mount Kosciuszko 2229 m

Population
Total: 19 731 000
Density: 3 persons per sq km

Settlement
% Urban population: 92
Main towns/cities: Sydney, Melbourne, Adelaide, Brisbane, Perth

Land use
Main crops: Wheat, sugar, rice, barley
Main industries: Food products, chemicals, transport equipment

Development indicators
Life expectancy: male 76, female 82
GNI per capita: US$ 19 740
Primary school enrolment ratio: 102
% Access to safe water: 100

Key

	3000 – 5000 m
	2000 – 3000 m
	1000 – 2000 m
	500 – 1000 m
	200 – 500 m
	0 – 200 m
	Ice cap
	Polar pack ice
	Drifting ice

Scale 1 : 35 000 000

WWW National Oceanic and Atmosphere Administration
www.noaa.gov

160°W 170°W 180° 170°E 160°E 150°E 140°E 130°E 120°E 110°E 100°E 90°E 80°E 70°E 60°E 50°E 40°E 30°E 20°E 10°E 0°
10°W 20°W 30°W 40°W 50°W 60°W 70°W 80°W 90°W 100°W 110°W 120°W 130°W 140°W 150°W

Bering Sea

Arctic Circle

Khrebet Kolymskiy

RUSSIAN FEDERATION

Wrangel Island

Verkhoyanskiy Khrebet

Brooks Range

U.S.A.

Mackenzie Mts

NORTH AMERICA

Beaufort Sea

East Siberian Sea

ARCTIC OCEAN

ASIA

Central Siberian Plateau

New Siberia Islands

Laptev Sea

Victoria Island

CANADA

Parry Islands

North Pole

Severnaya Zemlya

West Siberian Plain

Ellesmere Island

Zemlya Frantsa-Iosifa

Kara Sea

Baffin Island

Baffin Bay

80°N

Spitsbergen

Novaya Zemlya

GREENLAND (Denmark)

70°N

Barents Sea

EUROPE

Norwegian Sea

NORWAY

SWEDEN

FINLAND

Scandinavia

ICELAND

Arctic Circle

Cross section from A to B

metres
1000
sea level 0
1000
2000
3000
4000
5000

A CANADA

Beaufort Sea

Polar pack ice

North Pole

Drifting ice

Barents Sea

RUSSIAN FEDERATION B

Canada Basin

Alpha Ridge

Amundsen Basin

Nansen Basin

Arctic Circle

70°N

80°N

90°N

80°N

70°N

Arctic Circle

Polar Stereographic projection

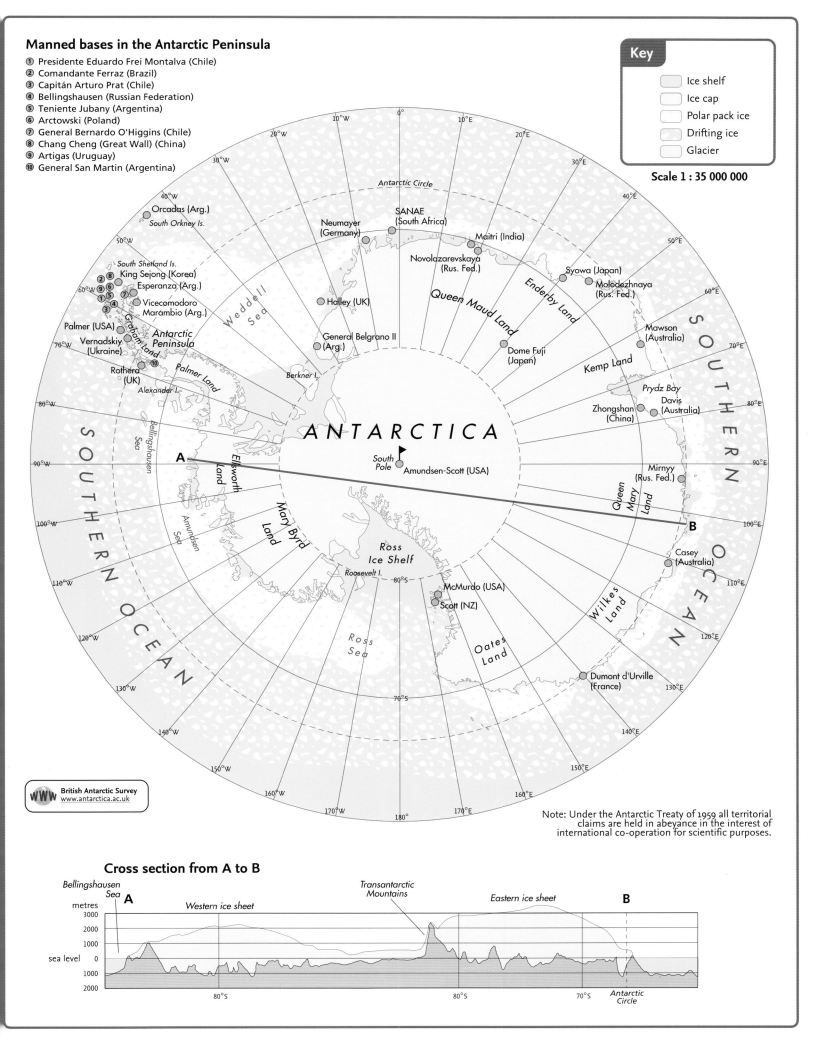

Manned bases in the Antarctic Peninsula

① Presidente Eduardo Frei Montalva (Chile)
② Comandante Ferraz (Brazil)
③ Capitán Arturo Prat (Chile)
④ Bellingshausen (Russian Federation)
⑤ Teniente Jubany (Argentina)
⑥ Arctowski (Poland)
⑦ General Bernardo O'Higgins (Chile)
⑧ Chang Cheng (Great Wall) (China)
⑨ Artigas (Uruguay)
⑩ General San Martin (Argentina)

Key
Ice shelf
Ice cap
Polar pack ice
Drifting ice
Glacier

Scale 1 : 35 000 000

Note: Under the Antarctic Treaty of 1959 all territorial claims are held in abeyance in the interest of international co-operation for scientific purposes.

British Antarctic Survey
www.antarctica.ac.uk

Cross section from A to B

Polar Stereographic projection

Key

- over 5000 m
- 3000 – 5000 m
- 2000 – 3000 m
- 1000 – 2000 m
- 500 – 1000 m
- 200 – 500 m
- 0 – 200 m
- land below sea level

- 0 – 200 m
- 200 – 4000 m
- 4000 – 6000 m
- over 6000 m

ARCTIC OCEAN

80°N · 160°W · 140°W · 120°W · 100°W · 80°W · 60°W · 40°W · 20°W

Ellesmere Island

Baffin Bay · Greenland

Victoria Island · Baffin Island

Arctic Circle · Great Bear Lake · Davis Str.

Yukon · Mt McKinley 6194 · Iceland

60°N · Great Slave Lake

Mt Logan 5959 · Canadian Shield · Cape Farewell · British Isles

Aleutian Is · Gulf of Alaska · Hudson Bay

Vancouver Island · Missouri · Lake Superior · Lake Huron · St Lawrence · Newfoundland

NORTH · Lake Michigan · Appalachian Mts

Great Plains · Ohio

AMERICA · Mississippi · North American Basin

7 · Mt Whitney 4418 · Colorado · Rio Grande

Hawaiian Islands · Sierra Madre · Bahamas · Canary Islands

Tropic of Cancer

20°N · ATLANTIC

Hawaii · Gulf of Mexico · Cuba · Greater Antilles · Hispaniola 8605 · Milwaukee Deep · Cape Verde Islands

Yucatan · Caribbean Sea

PACIFIC · Panama Canal · OCEAN · Fouta Djallon

6 · Line Is · Orinoco · Guiana Highlands

0° Equator · OCEAN · Galapagos Islands · Chimborazo 6310 · SOUTH · Amazon

Marquesas Islands · Madeira · Brazil Basin

5 · AMERICA · Tocantins · Brazilian

Society Is · Tuamotu Archipelago · Gran Chaco · Paraguay · Paraná · Highlands · St Hele

20°S · Peru-Chile Trench · Andes

Tropic of Capricorn · Pitcairn Island · Nevado Ojos del Salado

Easter Island · 6908 · Nevado Ojos del Salado

Tonga Trench · Cerro Aconcagua 6959 · Pampas

4 · Southwest Pacific Basin · Rio de la Plata · Tristan da Cu

Kermadec Trench

40°S · Patagonia · Argentine Basin

3 · Falkland Islands · South Georgia

Isla Grande Tierra del Fuego

C. Horn · Drake Passage

60°S · Southeast Pacific Basin · Antarctic Peninsula · Weddell Sea

Antarctic Circle

A 2 B C D E G H

80°S · 160°W · 140°W · 120°W · 100°W · 80°W · 60°W · 40°W · 20°W

Mountain heights	metres
Mt Everest (Nepal/China)	8848
K2 (Jammu & Kashmir/China)	8611
Kangchenjunga (Nepal/India)	8586
Dhaulagiri (Nepal)	8167
Annapurna (Nepal)	8091
Cerro Aconcagua (Argentina)	6959
Nevado Ojos del Salado (Arg./Chile)	6908
Chimborazo (Ecuador)	6310
Mt McKinley (USA)	6194
Mt Logan (Canada)	5959

Island areas	sq km
Greenland	2 175 600
New Guinea	808 510
Borneo	745 561
Madagascar	587 040
Baffin Island	507 451
Sumatra	473 606
Honshū	227 414
Great Britain	218 476
Victoria Island	217 291
Ellesmere Island	196 236

Continents and Oceans	sq km
Asia	45 036 492
Africa	30 343 578
North America	24 680 331
South America	17 815 420
Antarctica	12 093 000
Europe	9 908 599
Oceania	8 923 000
Pacific Ocean	166 241 000
Atlantic Ocean	86 557 000
Indian Ocean	73 427 000
Arctic Ocean	9 485 000

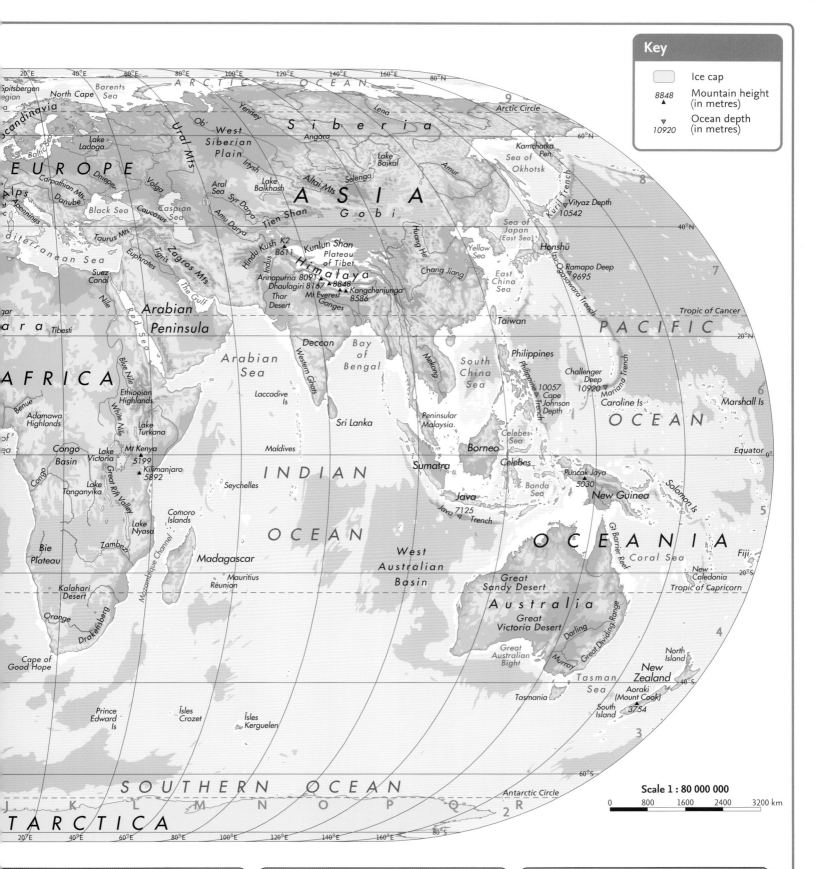

Key

⬜	Ice cap
8848 ▲	Mountain height (in metres)
▽ 10920	Ocean depth (in metres)

Scale 1 : 80 000 000

0   800   1600   2400   3200 km

Lake areas	sq km
Caspian Sea	371 795
Lake Superior	82 100
Lake Victoria	68 800
Lake Huron	59 600
Lake Michigan	57 800
Lake Tanganyika	32 900
Great Bear Lake	31 328
Lake Baikal	30 500
Lake Nyasa	30 044

River lengths	km
Nile (Africa)	6695
Amazon (S. America)	6516
Chang Jiang (Asia)	6380
Mississippi-Missouri (N. America)	5969
Ob'-Irtysh (Asia)	5568
Yenisey-Angara-Selenga (Asia)	5500
Huang He (Asia)	5464
Congo (Africa)	4667
Río de la Plata-Paraná (S. America)	4500
Mekong (Asia)	4425

World extremes	
Highest mountain	
Mt Everest (Asia)	8848 m
Largest inland water area	
Caspian Sea	371 795 sq km
Largest island	
Greenland	2 175 600 sq km
Longest river	
Nile (Africa)	6695 km
Deepest water	
Mariana Trench (Pacific Ocean)	10 920 m

Eckert IV projection

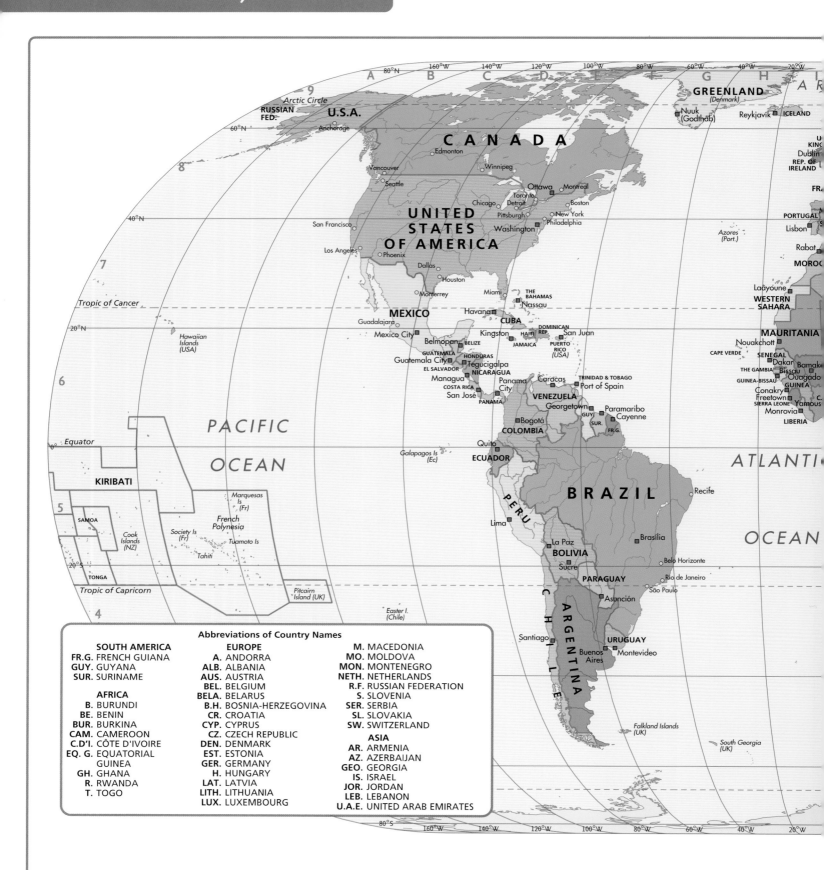

Abbreviations of Country Names

SOUTH AMERICA	EUROPE	M. MACEDONIA
FR.G. FRENCH GUIANA	A. ANDORRA	MO. MOLDOVA
GUY. GUYANA	ALB. ALBANIA	MON. MONTENEGRO
SUR. SURINAME	AUS. AUSTRIA	NETH. NETHERLANDS
	BEL. BELGIUM	R.F. RUSSIAN FEDERATION
AFRICA	BELA. BELARUS	S. SLOVENIA
B. BURUNDI	B.H. BOSNIA-HERZEGOVINA	SER. SERBIA
BE. BENIN	CR. CROATIA	SL. SLOVAKIA
BUR. BURKINA	CYP. CYPRUS	SW. SWITZERLAND
CAM. CAMEROON	CZ. CZECH REPUBLIC	ASIA
C.D'I. CÔTE D'IVOIRE	DEN. DENMARK	AR. ARMENIA
EQ. G. EQUATORIAL	EST. ESTONIA	AZ. AZERBAIJAN
GUINEA	GER. GERMANY	GEO. GEORGIA
GH. GHANA	H. HUNGARY	IS. ISRAEL
R. RWANDA	LAT. LATVIA	JOR. JORDAN
T. TOGO	LITH. LITHUANIA	LEB. LEBANON
	LUX. LUXEMBOURG	U.A.E. UNITED ARAB EMIRATES

Time Comparisons

Time varies around the world due to the earth's rotation causing different parts of the world to be in light or darkness at any one time. To account for this, the world is divided into twenty-four Standard Time Zones based on 15° intervals of longitude.

1:00am	2:00am	3:00am	4:00am	5:00am	6:00am	7:00am	8:00am	9:00am	10:00am	11:00am	noon
Samoa Tonga (next day)	Hawaiian Is Cook Is Tahiti	Anchorage	Vancouver Seattle Los Angeles	Edmonton Phoenix	Winnipeg Chicago Mexico City	New York Miami Lima	Puerto Rico La Paz Asunción	Nuuk Brasília Buenos Aires	South Georgia	Azores Cape Verde	Reykjav Londo Freetow

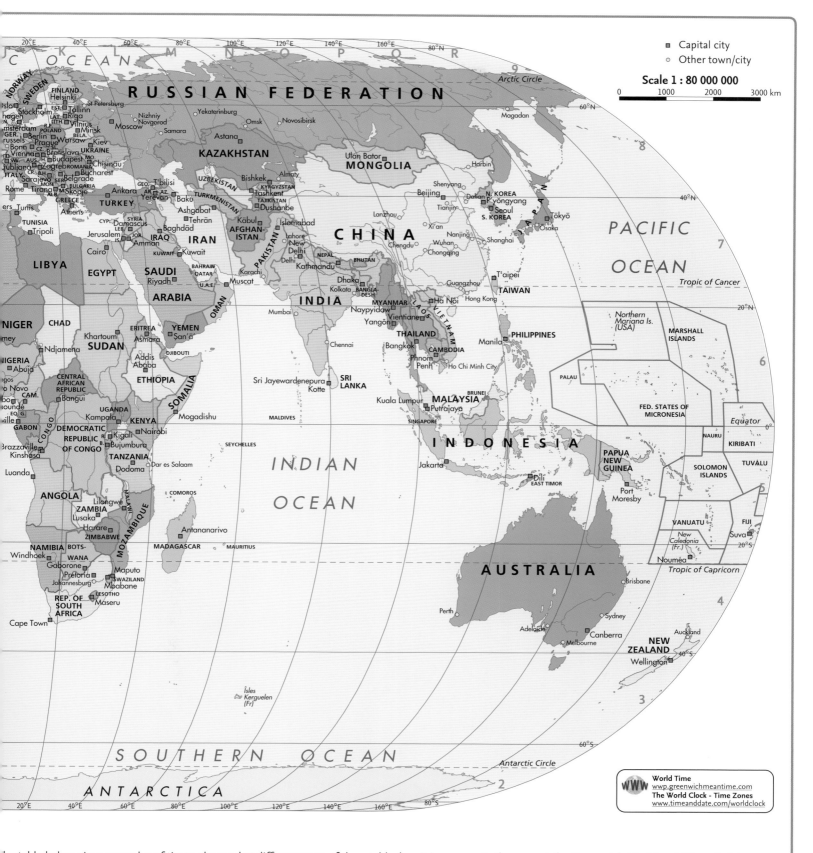

□ Capital city
○ Other town/city

Scale 1 : 80 000 000

0 1000 2000 3000 km

The table below gives examples of times observed at different parts of the world when it is 12 noon in the zone at the Greenwich Meridian (0° longitude). The time at 0° is known as Greenwich Mean Time (GMT).

...opm	2:00pm	3:00pm	4:00pm	5:00pm	6:00pm	7:00pm	8:00pm	9:00pm	10:00pm	11:00pm	midnight
Oslo Paris ...shasa	Helsinki Cairo Cape Town	St Petersburg Riyadh Dodoma	T'bilisi U.A.E. Mauritius	Yekaterinburg Tashkent Karachi	Omsk Almaty Dhaka	Ha Nôi Bangkok Jakarta	Ulan Bator Hong Kong Perth	P'yŏngyang Tōkyō Palau	Port Moresby Brisbane Canberra	Magadan Solomon Is New Caledonia	Marshall Is Fiji Wellington

Eckert IV projection

World Time
wwp.greenwichmeantime.com
The World Clock - Time Zones
www.timeanddate.com/worldclock

NORTH AMERICAN PLATE

JUAN DE FUCA PLATE

Mount St Helens

San Andreas Fault

Arctic Circle

Greenland

Hekla
Iceland
British Isles

PACIFIC PLATE

Hawaiian Islands
Kilauea

Tropic of Cancer

El Chichónal

Soufrière Hills

CARIBBEAN PLATE

COCOS PLATE

Nevado del Ruiz

Galeras

PACIFIC OCEAN

Equator

SOUTH AMERICAN PLATE

ATLANTIC OCEAN

NAZCA PLATE

Tropic of Capricorn

Volcán Llaima

ANTARCTICA

Antarctic Circle

Crustal plates

The earth is made up of three main layers.

The outer layer, known as the crust, ranges in thickness from a few kilometres under the oceans to almost 50 km under mountain ranges.

The middle layer, known as the mantle, makes up 82% of the earth's volume. At the centre (core) of the earth, temperatures reach 4300 °C.

——	Plate boundary
←——→	Direction of movement

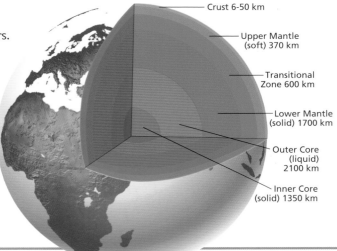

Crust 6-50 km

Upper Mantle (soft) 370 km

Transitional Zone 600 km

Lower Mantle (solid) 1700 km

Outer Core (liquid) 2100 km

Inner Core (solid) 1350 km

Earthquakes

Earthquakes occur most frequently along the junction of the plates which make up the earth's crust.

They are caused by the release of stress which builds up at the plate edges. When shock waves from these movements reach the surface they are felt as earthquakes which may result in severe damage to property or loss of lives.

● High magnitude earthquake (over 7.8 on Richter scale)

See page 36 for explanation of Richter scale

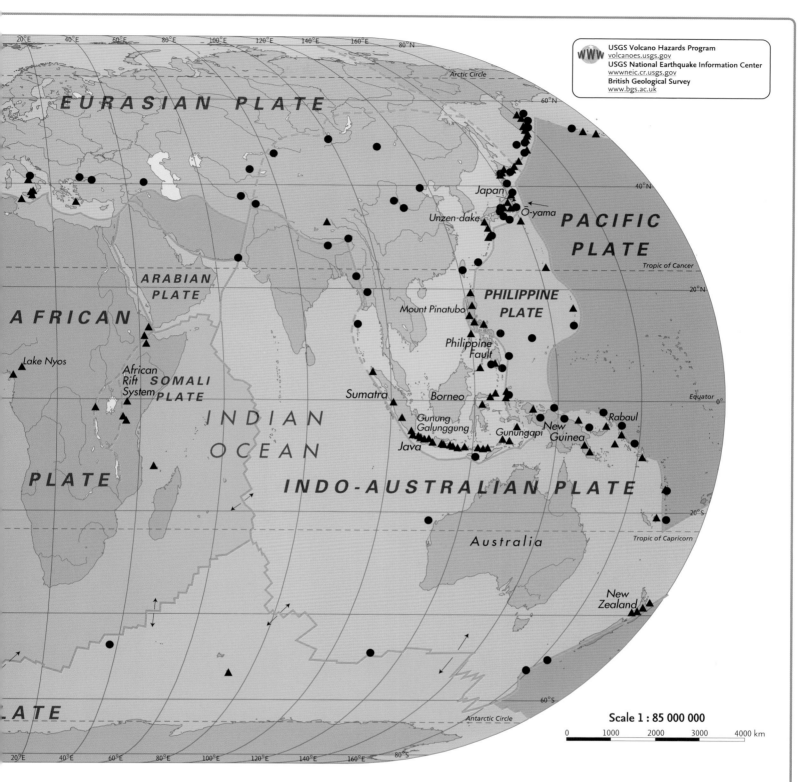

WWW USGS Volcano Hazards Program
volcanoes.usgs.gov
USGS National Earthquake Information Center
wwwneic.cr.usgs.gov
British Geological Survey
www.bgs.ac.uk

Scale 1 : 85 000 000

| 0 | 1000 | 2000 | 3000 | 4000 km |

Eckert IV projection

Year	Earthquake locations	Force	Deaths
1990	Manjil, Iran	7.7	50 000
1991	Uttar Pradesh, India	6.1	1600
1992	Flores, Indonesia	7.5	2500
1993	Maharashtra, India	6.4	9748
1995	Kōbe, Japan	7.2	5502
1995	Sakhalin, Russian Fed.	7.6	2500
1997	Quae'n, Iran	7.1	2400
1998	Afghanistan/Tajikistan	6.1, 6.9	6300
1998	Papua New Guinea	7.1	2183
1999	İzmit, Turkey	7.4	17 118
1999	Chi-Chi, Taiwan	7.6	2400
2001	Gujarat, India	6.9	20 085
2002	Hindu Kush, Afghanistan	6.0	1000
2003	Boumerdes, Algeria	5.8	2266
2003	Bam, Iran	6.6	26 271

Volcanoes

The greatest number of volcanoes are located in the 'Ring of Fire' around the Pacific Ocean.

Violent eruptions often occur when two plates collide and the heat generated forces molten rock (magma) upwards through weaknesses in the earth's crust.

Thousands of volcanic eruptions of varying intensity occur each year.

▲ Active volcano

Year	Volcano locations
1980	Mount St Helens, USA
1982	El Chichónal, Mexico
1982	Gunung Galunggung, Indonesia
1983	Kilauea, Hawaii
1983	Ō-yama, Japan
1985	Nevado del Ruiz, Colombia
1986	Lake Nyos, Cameroon
1991	Hekla, Iceland
1991	Mount Pinatubo, Philippines
1991	Unzen-dake, Japan
1993	Mayon, Philippines
1993	Galeras, Colombia
1994	Volcán Llaima, Chile
1994	Rabaul, Papua New Guinea
1997	Soufrière Hills, Montserrat

Climatic graphs

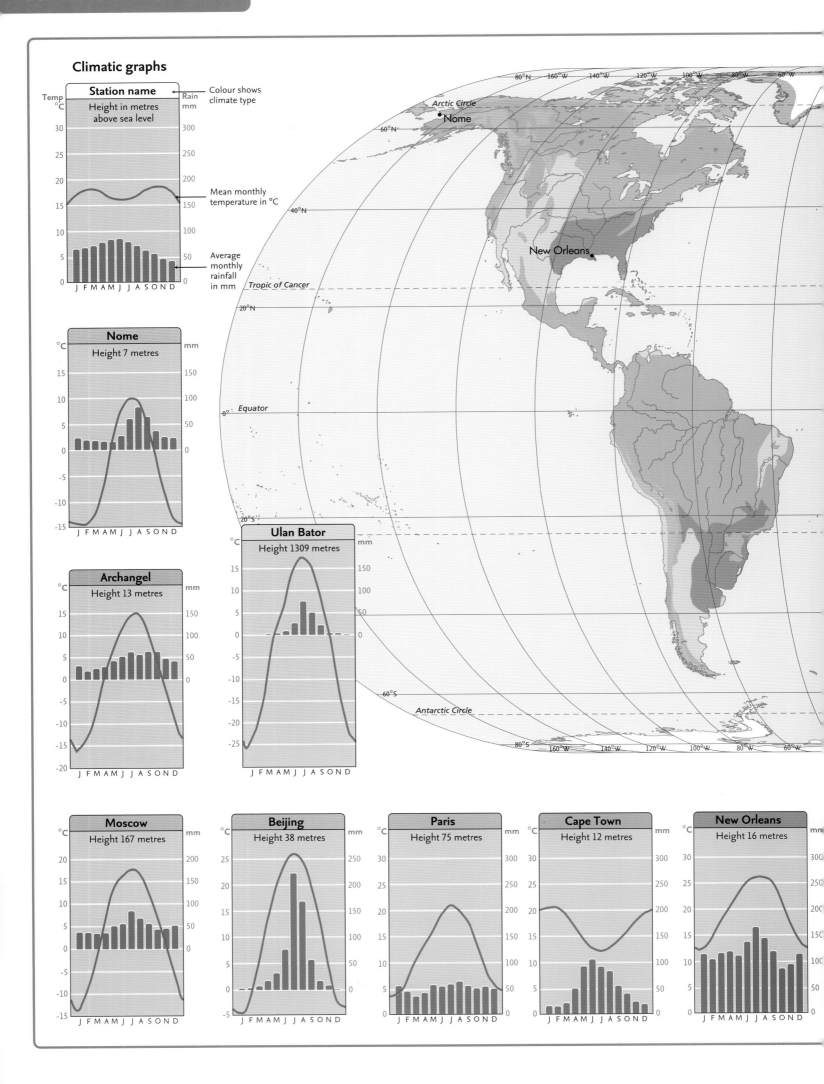

Station name

Temp °C — Height in metres above sea level — Rain mm

Colour shows climate type

Mean monthly temperature in °C

Average monthly rainfall in mm

Nome
Height 7 metres

Archangel
Height 13 metres

Ulan Bator
Height 1309 metres

Moscow
Height 167 metres

Beijing
Height 38 metres

Paris
Height 75 metres

Cape Town
Height 12 metres

New Orleans
Height 16 metres

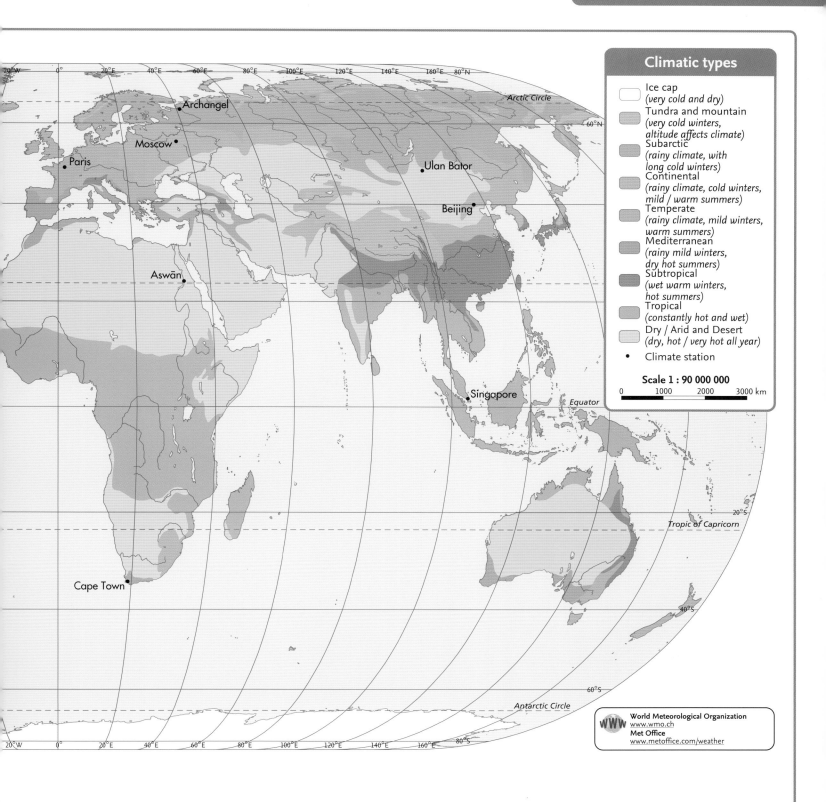

Climatic types

- Ice cap
  (very cold and dry)
- Tundra and mountain
  (very cold winters,
  altitude affects climate)
- Subarctic
  (rainy climate, with
  long cold winters)
- Continental
  (rainy climate, cold winters,
  mild / warm summers)
- Temperate
  (rainy climate, mild winters,
  warm summers)
- Mediterranean
  (rainy mild winters,
  dry hot summers)
- Subtropical
  (wet warm winters,
  hot summers)
- Tropical
  (constantly hot and wet)
- Dry / Arid and Desert
  (dry, hot / very hot all year)
- • Climate station

Scale 1 : 90 000 000

| 0 | 1000 | 2000 | 3000 km |

World Meteorological Organization
www.wmo.ch
Met Office
www.metoffice.com/weather

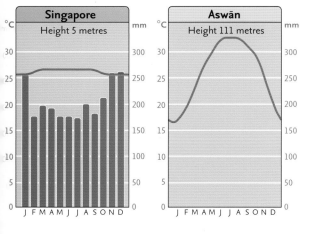

Climatic statistics

Nome	Jan	Feb	Mar	Apr	May	Jun	Jul	Aug	Sep	Oct	Nov	Dec
Temperature - °C	-15	-15	-13	-7	2	8	10	10	6	-2	-9	-14
Rainfall - mm	24	20	19	17	17	28	61	83	65	38	26	24

Beijing	Jan	Feb	Mar	Apr	May	Jun	Jul	Aug	Sep	Oct	Nov	Dec
Temperature - °C	-5	-2	5	14	20	24	26	25	20	13	4	-3
Rainfall - mm	4	5	8	18	33	78	224	170	58	18	9	3

Cape Town	Jan	Feb	Mar	Apr	May	Jun	Jul	Aug	Sep	Oct	Nov	Dec
Temperature - °C	21	21	20	17	15	13	12	13	14	16	18	20
Rainfall - mm	16	15	22	50	92	105	91	83	54	40	24	19

ARCTIC OCEAN

Arctic Circle

80°N

160°W

140°W

120°W

100°W

80°W

60°W

40°W

20°W

60°N

40°N

Tropic of Cancer

20°N

ATLANTIC

PACIFIC

OCEAN

OCEAN

0° Equator

OCEAN

20°S

Tropic of Capricorn

40°S

60°S

Antarctic Circle

80°S

160°W

140°W

120°W

100°W

80°W

60°W

40°W

20°W

Ice cap and ice shelf
Extremely cold. No vegetation.

Tundra
Arctic tundra
Very cold climate. Simple vegetation such as mosses, lichens, grasses and flowering herbs.

Mountain/Alpine
Very low night-time temperatures. Only a few dwarf trees and small leafed shrubs can grow.

Grassland
Savanna grassland
Warm or hot climate. Tropical grasslands with scattered thorn bushes or trees.

Temperate grassland
Grassland is the main vegetation. Summers are hot and winters cold.

Mediterranean
Mild winters and dry summers. Vegetation is mixed shrubs and herbaceous plants.

Desert
Hot with little rainfall. Very sparse vegetation except cacti and grasses adapted to the harsh conditions.

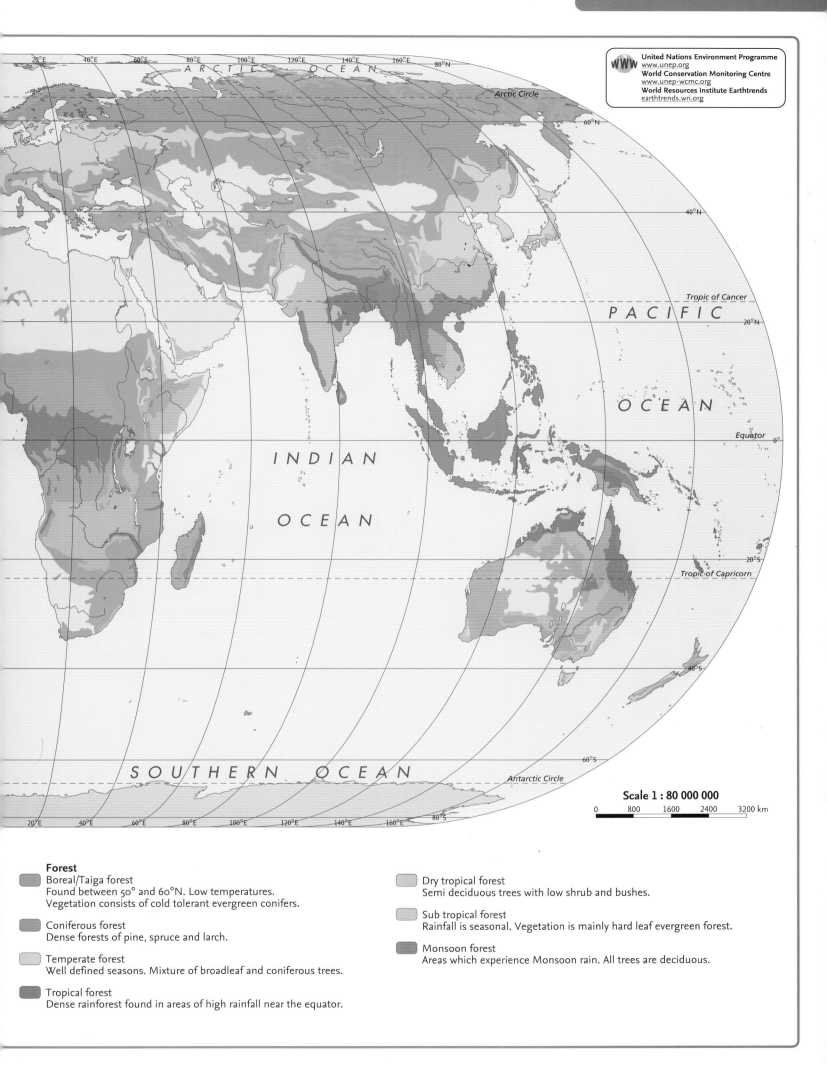

WWW United Nations Environment Programme
www.unep.org
World Conservation Monitoring Centre
www.unep-wcmc.org
World Resources Institute Earthtrends
earthtrends.wri.org

ARCTIC OCEAN

Arctic Circle

60°N

40°N

Tropic of Cancer

PACIFIC

20°N

OCEAN

Equator 0°

INDIAN

OCEAN

20°S

Tropic of Capricorn

40°S

60°S

SOUTHERN OCEAN

Antarctic Circle

Scale 1 : 80 000 000

| 0 | 800 | 1600 | 2400 | 3200 km |

80°S

Forest

Boreal/Taiga forest
Found between 50° and 60°N. Low temperatures.
Vegetation consists of cold tolerant evergreen conifers.

Coniferous forest
Dense forests of pine, spruce and larch.

Temperate forest
Well defined seasons. Mixture of broadleaf and coniferous trees.

Tropical forest
Dense rainforest found in areas of high rainfall near the equator.

Dry tropical forest
Semi deciduous trees with low shrub and bushes.

Sub tropical forest
Rainfall is seasonal. Vegetation is mainly hard leaf evergreen forest.

Monsoon forest
Areas which experience Monsoon rain. All trees are deciduous.

Eckert IV projection

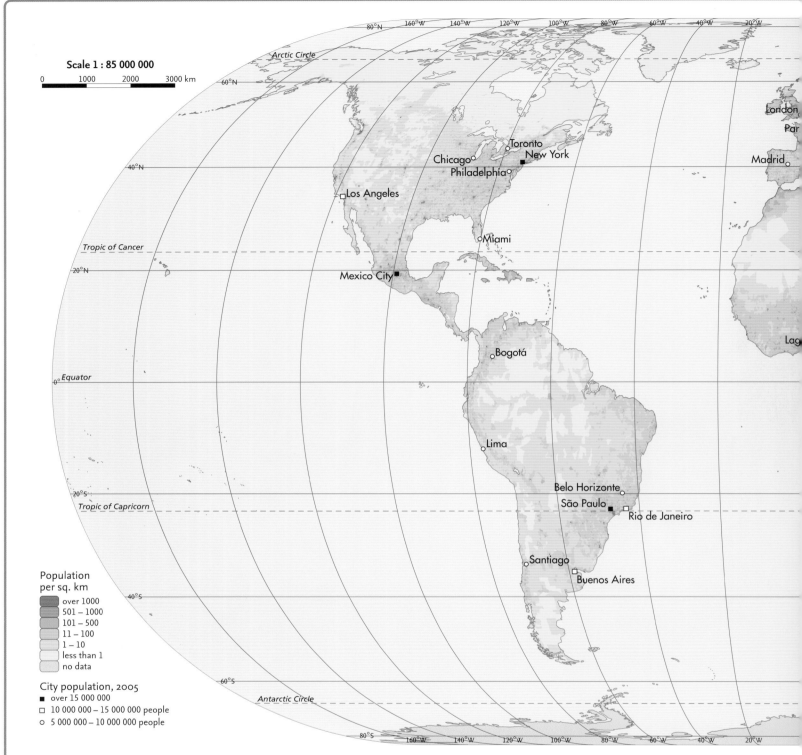

Scale 1 : 85 000 000

0   1000   2000   3000 km

Arctic Circle

Tropic of Cancer

Equator

Tropic of Capricorn

Antarctic Circle

Toronto
New York
Chicago
Philadelphia
Los Angeles
Miami
Mexico City
Bogotá
Lima
Belo Horizonte
São Paulo
Rio de Janeiro
Santiago
Buenos Aires
London
Par
Madrid
Lag
Lag

Population per sq. km

- over 1000
- 501 – 1000
- 101 – 500
- 11 – 100
- 1 – 10
- less than 1
- no data

City population, 2005

- ■ over 15 000 000
- □ 10 000 000 – 15 000 000 people
- ○ 5 000 000 – 10 000 000 people

World population distribution by continents

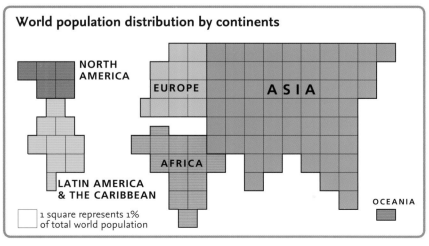

NORTH AMERICA

EUROPE

ASIA

AFRICA

LATIN AMERICA & THE CARIBBEAN

OCEANIA

☐ 1 square represents 1% of total world population

Country populations, 2003	
China, *Asia*	1 289 161 000
India, *Asia*	1 065 462 000
USA, *North America*	294 043 000
Indonesia, *Asia*	219 883 000
Brazil, *South America*	178 470 000
Pakistan, *Asia*	153 578 000
Bangladesh, *Asia*	146 736 000
Russian Federation, *Asia/Europe*	143 246 000
Japan, *Asia*	127 654 000
Nigeria, *Africa*	124 009 000
Mexico, *North America*	103 457 000
Germany, *Europe*	82 476 000
Vietnam, *Asia*	81 377 000
Philippines, *Asia*	79 999 000
Egypt, *Africa*	71 931 000

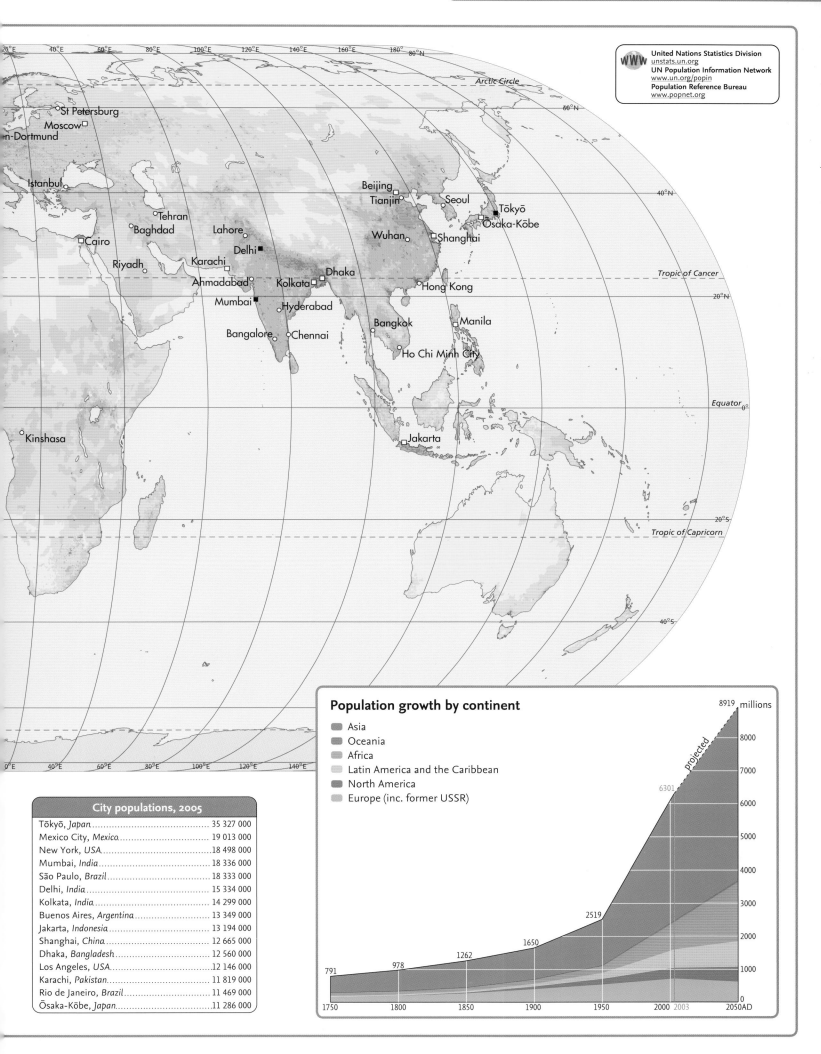

WWW United Nations Statistics Division
unstats.un.org
UN Population Information Network
www.un.org/popin
Population Reference Bureau
www.popnet.org

St Petersburg
Moscow
n-Dortmund
Istanbul
Tehran
Baghdad
Cairo
Riyadh
Karachi
Ahmadabad
Mumbai
Bangalore
Kinshasa
Lahore
Delhi
Kolkata
Dhaka
Hyderabad
Chennai
Beijing
Tianjin
Wuhan
Seoul
Tōkyō
Ōsaka-Kōbe
Shanghai
Hong Kong
Bangkok
Manila
Ho Chi Minh City
Jakarta

Arctic Circle
Tropic of Cancer
Equator
Tropic of Capricorn

80°N
60°N
40°N
20°N
0°
20°S
40°S

20°E 40°E 60°E 80°E 100°E 120°E 140°E 160°E 180° 80°N

City populations, 2005	
Tōkyō, *Japan*	35 327 000
Mexico City, *Mexico*	19 013 000
New York, *USA*	18 498 000
Mumbai, *India*	18 336 000
São Paulo, *Brazil*	18 333 000
Delhi, *India*	15 334 000
Kolkata, *India*	14 299 000
Buenos Aires, *Argentina*	13 349 000
Jakarta, *Indonesia*	13 194 000
Shanghai, *China*	12 665 000
Dhaka, *Bangladesh*	12 560 000
Los Angeles, *USA*	12 146 000
Karachi, *Pakistan*	11 819 000
Rio de Janeiro, *Brazil*	11 469 000
Ōsaka-Kōbe, *Japan*	11 286 000

Population growth by continent

- Asia
- Oceania
- Africa
- Latin America and the Caribbean
- North America
- Europe (inc. former USSR)

8919 millions

projected

6301

2519

1650

1262

978

791

8000
7000
6000
5000
4000
3000
2000
1000
0

1750 1800 1850 1900 1950 2000 2003 2050AD

Eckert IV projection

Flag	Country	Capital city	Area sq km	Total population 2003	Density persons per sq km 2003	Birth rate per 1000 population 2002	Life expectancy in years 2002	Population change average % per annum 2000-2005	Urban population % 2002
	Afghanistan	Kābul	652 225	23 897 000	37	49	43	3.9	23
	Albania	Tirana	28 748	3 166 000	110	17	74	0.7	44
	Algeria	Algiers	2 381 741	31 800 000	13	22	71	1.7	58
	Angola	Luanda	1 246 700	13 625 000	11	47	47	3.2	36
	Antigua & Barbuda	St John's	442	73 000	165	...	...	0.5	37
	Argentina	Buenos Aires	2 766 889	38 428 000	14	19	74	1.2	89
	Armenia	Yerevan	29 800	3 061 000	103	12	75	-0.5	67
	Australia	Canberra	7 692 024	19 731 000	3	13	79	1.0	92
	Austria	Vienna	83 855	8 116 000	97	9	79	0.1	68
	Azerbaijan	Baku	86 600	8 370 000	97	16	65	0.9	52
	Bahamas, The	Nassau	13 939	314 000	23	18	70	1.1	89
	Bahrain	Manama	691	724 000	1 048	21	73	2.2	93
	Bangladesh	Dhaka	143 998	146 736 000	1 019	28	62	2.0	26
	Barbados	Bridgetown	430	270 000	628	14	75	0.4	51
	Belarus	Minsk	207 600	9 895 000	48	9	68	-0.5	70
	Belgium	Brussels	30 520	10 318 000	338	10	79	0.2	98
	Belize	Belmopan	22 965	256 000	11	25	74	2.1	48
	Benin	Porto-Novo	112 620	6 736 000	60	38	53	2.7	44
	Bhutan	Thimphu	46 620	2 257 000	48	37	63	3.0	8
	Bolivia	La Paz/Sucre	1 098 581	8 808 000	8	29	64	1.9	63
	Bosnia & Herzegovina	Sarajevo	51 130	4 161 000	81	12	74	1.1	44
	Botswana	Gaborone	581 370	1 785 000	3	30	38	0.9	50
	Brazil	Brasília	8 514 879	178 470 000	21	19	69	1.2	82
	Brunei	Bandar Seri Begawan	5 765	358 000	62	19	77	2.3	73
	Bulgaria	Sofia	110 994	7 897 000	71	9	72	-0.9	68
	Burkina	Ouagadougou	274 200	13 002 000	47	43	43	3.0	17
	Burundi	Bujumbura	27 835	6 825 000	245	39	42	3.1	10
	Cambodia	Phnom Penh	181 000	14 144 000	78	27	54	2.4	18
	Cameroon	Yaoundé	475 442	16 018 000	34	36	48	1.8	50
	Canada	Ottawa	9 984 670	31 510 000	3	11	79	0.8	79
	Cape Verde	Praia	4 033	463 000	115	31	69	2.0	64
	Central African Republic	Bangui	622 436	3 865 000	6	36	42	1.3	42
	Chad	Ndjamena	1 284 000	8 598 000	7	45	48	3.0	25
	Chile	Santiago	756 945	15 805 000	21	16	76	1.2	86
	China	Beijing	9 562 000	1 304 196 000	135	15	71	0.7	38
	Colombia	Bogotá	1 141 748	44 222 000	39	21	72	1.6	76
	Comoros	Moroni	1 862	768 000	412	32	61	2.8	34
	Congo	Brazzaville	342 000	3 724 000	11	41	52	2.6	67
	Congo, Dem. Rep. of	Kinshasa	2 345 410	52 771 000	22	45	45	2.9	
	Costa Rica	San José	51 100	4 173 000	82	20	78	1.9	60
	Côte d'Ivoire	Yamoussoukro	322 463	16 631 000	52	37	45	1.6	45
	Croatia	Zagreb	56 538	4 428 000	78	10	74	-0.2	59
	Cuba	Havana	110 860	11 300 000	102	12	77	0.3	76
	Cyprus	Nicosia	9 251	802 000	87	13	78	0.8	71
	Czech Republic	Prague	78 864	10 236 000	130	9	75	-0.1	75
	Denmark	Copenhagen	43 075	5 364 000	125	12	77	0.2	85
	Djibouti	Djibouti	23 200	703 000	30	36	44	1.6	84

... no data available

Flag	Country	Capital city	Area sq km	Total population 2003	Density persons per sq km 2003	Birth rate per 1000 population 2002	Life expectancy in years 2002	Population change average % per annum 2000-2005	Urban population % 2002
	Dominica	Roseau	750	79 000	105	18	77	0.3	72
	Dominican Republic	Santo Domingo	48 442	8 745 000	181	23	67	1.5	67
	East Timor	Dili	14 874	778 000	52	43	...	4.0	8
	Ecuador	Quito	272 045	13 003 000	48	24	70	1.5	64
	Egypt	Cairo	1 000 250	71 931 000	72	24	69	2.0	43
	El Salvador	San Salvador	21 041	6 515 000	310	26	70	1.6	62
	Equatorial Guinea	Malabo	28 051	494 000	18	41	52	2.7	50
	Eritrea	Asmara	117 400	4 141 000	35	38	51	3.7	20
	Estonia	Tallinn	45 200	1 323 000	29	9	71	-1.1	70
	Ethiopia	Addis Ababa	1 133 880	70 678 000	62	42	42	2.5	16
	Fiji	Suva	18 330	839 000	46	22	70	1.0	51
	Finland	Helsinki	338 145	5 207 000	15	11	78	0.2	59
	France	Paris	543 965	60 144 000	111	13	79	0.5	76
	Gabon	Libreville	267 667	1 329 000	5	35	53	1.8	83
	Gambia, The	Banjul	11 295	1 426 000	126	37	53	2.7	32
	Georgia	T'bilisi	69 700	5 126 000	74	8	73	-0.9	57
	Germany	Berlin	357 022	82 476 000	231	9	78	0.1	88
	Ghana	Accra	238 537	20 922 000	88	29	55	2.2	37
	Greece	Athens	131 957	10 976 000	83	9	78	0.1	61
	Grenada	St George's	378	80 000	212	25	73	-0.3	39
	Guatemala	Guatemala City	108 890	12 347 000	113	33	65	2.6	40
	Guinea	Conakry	245 857	8 480 000	34	38	46	1.6	28
	Guinea-Bissau	Bissau	36 125	1 493 000	41	39	45	3.0	33
	Guyana	Georgetown	214 969	765 000	4	22	62	0.2	37
	Haiti	Port-au-Prince	27 750	8 326 000	300	32	52	1.3	37
	Honduras	Tegucigalpa	112 088	6 941 000	62	30	66	2.3	55
	Hungary	Budapest	93 030	9 877 000	106	10	72	-0.5	65
	Iceland	Reykjavík	102 820	290 000	3	13	80	0.8	93
	India	New Delhi	3 064 898	1 065 462 000	348	24	63	1.5	28
	Indonesia	Jakarta	1 919 445	219 883 000	115	20	67	1.3	43
	Iran	Tehrān	1 648 000	68 920 000	42	22	69	1.2	65
	Iraq	Baghdād	438 317	25 175 000	57	29	63	2.7	68
	Ireland	Dublin	70 282	3 956 000	56	14	77	1.1	60
	Israel	*Jerusalem	20 770	6 433 000	310	20	79	2.0	92
	Italy	Rome	301 245	57 423 000	191	9	78	-0.1	67
	Jamaica	Kingston	10 991	2 651 000	241	20	76	0.9	57
	Japan	Tōkyō	377 727	127 654 000	338	9	81	0.1	79
	Jordan	'Ammān	89 206	5 473 000	61	28	72	2.7	79
	Kazakhstan	Astana	2 717 300	15 433 000	6	15	62	-0.4	56
	Kenya	Nairobi	582 646	31 987 000	55	35	46	1.5	35
	Kiribati	Bairiki	717	88 000	123	28	63	1.4	39
	Kuwait	Kuwait	17 818	2 521 000	141	20	77	3.5	96
	Kyrgyzstan	Bishkek	198 500	5 138 000	26	19	65	1.4	34
	Laos	Vientiane	236 800	5 657 000	24	36	55	2.3	20
	Latvia	Rīga	63 700	2 307 000	36	8	70	-0.9	60
	Lebanon	Beirut	10 452	3 653 000	350	19	71	1.6	90
	Lesotho	Maseru	30 355	1 802 000	59	31	43	0.1	30

*Jerusalem - not internationally recognised.   ... no data available

Flag	Country	Capital city	Area sq km	Total population 2003	Density persons per sq km 2003	Birth rate per 1000 population 2002	Life expectancy in years 2002	Population change average % per annum 2000-2005	Urban population % 2002
	Liberia	Monrovia	111 369	3 367 000	30	43	47	4.1	46
	Libya	Tripoli	1 759 540	5 551 000	3	27	72	1.9	88
	Liechtenstein	Vaduz	160	34 000	213	...	...	0.9	22
	Lithuania	Vilnius	65 200	3 444 000	53	10	73	-0.6	69
	Luxembourg	Luxembourg	2 586	453 000	175	12	77	1.3	92
	Macedonia	Skopje	25 713	2 056 000	80	13	73	0.5	60
	Madagascar	Antananarivo	587 041	17 404 000	30	39	55	2.8	31
	Malawi	Lilongwe	118 484	12 105 000	102	45	38	2.0	16
	Malaysia	Kuala Lumpur/Putrajaya	332 965	24 425 000	73	22	73	1.9	59
	Maldives	Male	298	318 000	1 067	29	69	3.0	29
	Mali	Bamako	1 240 140	13 007 000	10	46	41	3.0	32
	Malta	Valletta	316	394 000	1 247	12	78	0.4	91
	Marshall Islands	Dalap-Uliga-Darrit	181	53 000	293	...	...	1.2	66
	Mauritania	Nouakchott	1 030 700	2 893 000	3	40	51	3.0	60
	Mauritius	Port Louis	2 040	1 221 000	599	17	73	1.0	42
	Mexico	Mexico City	1 972 545	103 457 000	52	22	74	1.5	75
	Micronesia	Palikir	701	109 000	155	25	69	0.8	29
	Moldova	Chișinău	33 700	4 267 000	127	11	67	-0.1	42
	Mongolia	Ulan Bator	1 565 000	2 594 000	2	23	65	1.3	57
	Montenegro	Podgorica	13 812	620 145	45	12	73	-0.1	52
	Morocco	Rabat	446 550	30 566 000	68	21	68	1.6	57
	Mozambique	Maputo	799 380	18 863 000	24	40	41	1.8	34
	Myanmar	Yangôn/Naypyidaw	676 577	49 485 000	73	23	57	1.3	29
	Namibia	Windhoek	824 292	1 987 000	2	35	42	1.4	32
	Nepal	Kathmandu	147 181	25 164 000	171	32	60	2.2	13
	Netherlands	Amsterdam/The Hague	41 526	16 149 000	389	12	78	0.5	90
	New Zealand	Wellington	270 534	3 875 000	14	14	78	0.8	86
	Nicaragua	Managua	130 000	5 466 000	42	29	69	2.4	57
	Niger	Niamey	1 267 000	11 972 000	9	49	46	3.6	22
	Nigeria	Abuja	923 768	124 009 000	134	39	45	2.5	46
	North Korea	P'yŏngyang	120 538	22 664 000	188	18	62	0.5	61
	Norway	Oslo	323 878	4 533 000	14	13	79	0.4	75
	Oman	Muscat	309 500	2 851 000	9	26	74	2.9	77
	Pakistan	Islamabad	803 940	153 578 000	191	33	64	2.4	34
	Palau	Melekeok	497	20 000	40	...	...	2.1	70
	Panama	Panama City	77 082	3 120 000	40	20	75	1.8	57
	Papua New Guinea	Port Moresby	462 840	5 711 000	12	32	57	2.2	18
	Paraguay	Asunción	406 752	5 878 000	14	30	71	2.4	57
	Peru	Lima	1 285 216	27 167 000	21	22	70	1.5	74
	Philippines	Manila	300 000	79 999 000	267	26	70	1.8	60
	Poland	Warsaw	312 683	38 587 000	123	10	74	-0.1	63
	Portugal	Lisbon	88 940	10 062 000	113	11	76	0.1	67
	Qatar	Doha	11 437	610 000	53	14	75	1.5	93
	Romania	Bucharest	237 500	22 334 000	94	10	70	-0.2	56
	Russian Federation	Moscow	17 075 400	143 246 000	8	10	66	-0.6	73
	Rwanda	Kigali	26 338	8 387 000	318	44	40	2.2	6
	St Kitts & Nevis	Basseterre	261	42 000	161	17	71	-0.3	35

... no data available

Flag	Country	Capital city	Area sq km	Total population 2003	Density persons per sq km 2003	Birth rate per 1000 population 2002	Life expectancy in years 2002	Population change average % per annum 2000-2005	Urban population % 2002
	St Lucia	Castries	616	149 000	242	19	72	0.8	38
	St Vincent & the Grenadines	Kingstown	389	120 000	308	18	73	0.6	57
	Samoa	Apia	2 831	178 000	63	29	69	1.0	23
	São Tomé & Príncipe	São Tomé	964	161 000	167	31	66	2.5	48
	Saudi Arabia	Riyadh	2 200 000	24 217 000	11	32	73	2.9	87
	Senegal	Dakar	196 720	10 095 000	51	35	52	2.4	49
	Serbia	Belgrade	88 361	9 379 437	106	12	73	-0.1	52
	Seychelles	Victoria	455	81 000	178	19	73	0.9	65
	Sierra Leone	Freetown	71 740	4 971 000	69	44	37	3.8	38
	Singapore	Singapore	639	4 253 000	6 656	12	...	1.7	100
	Slovakia	Bratislava	49 035	5 402 000	110	11	73	0.1	58
	Slovenia	Ljubljana	20 251	1 984 000	98	9	76	-0.1	49
	Solomon Islands	Honiara	28 370	477 000	17	39	69	2.9	21
	Somalia	Mogadishu	637 657	9 890 000	16	50	47	4.2	28
	South Africa, Republic of	Pretoria/Cape Town	1 219 080	45 026 000	37	25	46	0.6	58
	South Korea	Seoul	99 274	47 700 000	480	12	74	0.6	83
	Spain	Madrid	504 782	41 060 000	81	10	78	0.2	78
	Sri Lanka	Sri Jayewardenepura Kotte	65 610	19 065 000	291	18	74	0.8	23
	Sudan	Khartoum	2 505 813	33 610 000	13	33	58	2.2	38
	Suriname	Paramaribo	163 820	436 000	3	21	70	0.8	75
	Swaziland	Mbabane	17 364	1 077 000	62	35	44	0.8	27
	Sweden	Stockholm	449 964	8 876 000	20	11	80	0.1	83
	Switzerland	Bern	41 293	7 169 000	174	9	80	-0.1	68
	Syria	Damascus	185 180	17 800 000	96	29	70	2.4	52
	Taiwan	T'aipei	36 179	22 548 000	623	...	...	...	...
	Tajikistan	Dushanbe	143 100	6 245 000	44	23	67	0.9	28
	Tanzania	Dodoma	945 087	36 977 000	39	38	43	1.9	34
	Thailand	Bangkok	513 115	62 833 000	122	15	69	1.0	20
	Togo	Lomé	56 785	4 909 000	86	34	50	2.3	35
	Tonga	Nuku'alofa	748	104 000	139	23	71	1.0	33
	Trinidad & Tobago	Port of Spain	5 130	1 303 000	254	16	72	0.3	75
	Tunisia	Tunis	164 150	9 832 000	60	18	73	1.1	67
	Turkey	Ankara	779 452	71 325 000	92	20	70	1.4	67
	Turkmenistan	Ashgabat	488 100	4 867 000	10	20	65	1.5	45
	Tuvalu	Vaiaku	25	11 000	440	...	...	1.2	...
	Uganda	Kampala	241 038	25 827 000	107	44	43	3.2	15
	Ukraine	Kiev	603 700	48 523 000	80	9	68	-0.8	68
	United Arab Emirates	Abu Dhabi	77 700	2 995 000	39	17	75	1.9	88
	United Kingdom	London	243 609	59 251 000	241	11	77	0.3	90
	United States of America	Washington	9 826 635	294 043 000	30	14	78	1.0	78
	Uruguay	Montevideo	176 215	3 415 000	19	16	75	0.7	92
	Uzbekistan	Tashkent	447 400	26 093 000	58	20	67	1.5	37
	Vanuatu	Port Vila	12 190	212 000	17	32	69	2.4	23
	Venezuela	Caracas	912 050	25 699 000	28	23	74	1.9	87
	Vietnam	Ha Nôi	329 565	81 377 000	247	19	70	1.4	25
	Yemen	Şan'ā'	527 968	20 010 000	38	41	57	3.5	25
	Zambia	Lusaka	752 614	10 812 000	14	39	37	1.2	40
	Zimbabwe	Harare	390 759	12 891 000	33	29	39	0.5	37

... no data available

The important names on the reference maps in the atlas are found in the index. The names are listed in alphabetical order. Each entry gives the country or region of the world in which the name is located followed by the page number, its alphanumeric grid reference and then its co-ordinates of latitude and longitude. Names of very large areas may have these co-ordinates omitted. Area names which are included in the index are referenced to the centre of the feature. In the case of rivers, the mouth or confluence is taken as the point of reference. It is therefore necessary to follow the river upstream from this point to find its name on the map.

On the map of part of Ireland to the right Dublin is found in grid square C3 at latitude 53° 21'N longitude 6° 18'W.

This appears in the index as Dublin Rep. of Ire. 11 C3 53.21N 6.18W. The chart below explains all the elements listed for each entry.

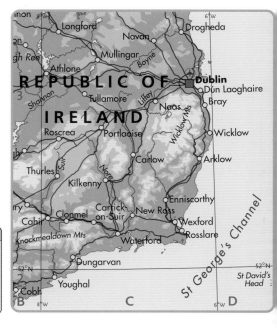

Dublin	Rep. of Ireland	11	C3	53.21N	6.18W
Name of the feature to be located.	Name of the country in which the feature is situated.	Page in the atlas where the feature is shown on the largest scale.	Grid square where the feature is found.	Degrees and minutes north or south of the equator.	Degrees and minutes east or west of Greenwich meridian.

Sometimes an abbreviated description of a feature is included in the entry. A list of abbreviations used in the index is included below.

Abbreviations

Afghan.	Afghanistan	Equat. Guinea	Equatorial Guinea	*mts.*, **Mts.**	mountains	R.S.A.	Republic of South Africa
Austa.	Australasia	*est.*	estuary	N. America	North America	Russian Fed.	Russian Federation
b., **B.**	bay, Bay	*f.*	physical feature eg. valley, plain	Neth.	Netherlands	Serb.	Serbia
Bangla.	Bangladesh			N. Korea	North Korea	S. America	South America
Bosnia.	Bosnia-Herzegovina	**G.**	Gulf	**Oc.**	Ocean	S. Korea	South Korea
c., **C.**	cape, Cape	I.o.M	Isle of Man	*Pen.*, **Pen.**	peninsula, Peninsula	*str.*, **Str.**	strait, Strait
C. America	Central America	*l.* **L.**	lake, Lake	Phil.	Philippines	Switz.	Switzerland
C.A.R.	Central African Republic	Lux.	Luxembourg	P.N.G.	Papua New Guinea	U.K.	United Kingdom
d.	Internal division eg. state, county	**Mont.**	Montenegro	*r.*	river	U.S.A.	United States of America
		Mt.	Mount	Rep. of Ire.	Republic of Ireland	W. Sahara	Western Sahara
des.	desert	*mtn.*	mountain	*resr.*	Reservoir		

A

Aberdeen Scotland **10 E5** 57.08N 2.07W
Aberystwyth Wales **11 D3** 52.25N 4.06W
Abidjan Côte d'Ivoire **42 C5** 5.19N 4.01W
Abu Dhabi U.A.E. **30 E3** 24.27N 54.23E
Abuja Nigeria **42 D5** 9.12N 7.11E
Acapulco Mexico **53 J4** 16.51N 99.56W
Accra Ghana **42 C5** 5.33N 0.15W
Aconcagua, Cerro *mtn.* Argentina **57 D3** 32.37S 70.00W
Adamawa Highlands Nigeria/Cameroon **42 E5** 7.05N 12.00E
Adana Turkey **21 G2** 37.00N 35.19E
Addis Ababa Ethiopia **42 G5** 9.03N 38.42E
Adelaide Australia **64 D2** 34.56S 138.36E
Aden, G. of Indian Oc. **30 D2** 13.00N 50.00E
Adriatic Sea Med. Sea **22 F5** 42.30N 16.00E
Aegean Sea Med. Sea **20 F2** 39.00N 25.00E
Afghanistan Asia **30 F4** 33.00N 65.30E
Africa 42-43
Ahmadabad India **31 G3** 23.03N 72.40E
Albania Europe **20 E3** 41.00N 20.00E
Aleppo Syria **30 C4** 36.14N 37.10E
Alexandria Egypt **42 F8** 31.13N 29.55E
Algeria Africa **42 C7** 28.00N 2.00E
Algiers Algeria **42 D8** 36.50N 3.00E
Alice Springs Australia **64 D3** 23.42S 133.52E
Allier *r.* France **20 D3** 46.58N 3.04E
Alps *mts.* Europe **20 D3** 46.00N 7.30E
Altai Mts. Mongolia **32 B8** 46.30N 93.30E
Altiplano *f.* Bolivia **58 C4** 18.00S 67.30W
Amazon *r.* Brazil **58 F7** 2.00S 50.00W
Amazon, Mouths of the *f.* Brazil **58 G8** 0.00 50.00W
'Ammān Jordan **30 C4** 31.57N 35.56E
Amsterdam Neth. **20 D4** 52.22N 4.54E
Amur *r.* Russian Fed. **28 J6** 53.17N 140.00E
Anápolis Brazil **58 G4** 16.19S 48.58W
Anchorage U.S.A. **52 E9** 61.10N 150.00W
Andaman Is. India **31 I2** 12.00N 93.00E
Andaman Sea Indian Oc. **31 I2** 11.00N 96.00E
Andes *mts.* S. America **56 D5** 15.00S 74.00W
Andorra Europe **20 D3** 42.30N 1.32E
Angola Africa **43 E3** 12.00S 18.00E
Ankara Turkey **21 G2** 39.55N 32.50E
Anshan China **32 E8** 41.05N 122.58E

Antananarivo Madagascar **43 H3** 18.52S 47.30E
Antarctica 69
Antigua and Barbuda Lesser Antilles **56 E8** 17.30N 61.49W
Antofagasta Chile **57 D4** 23.40S 70.23W
Aoraki *mtn.* New Zealand **65 H1** 43.36S 170.09E
Apennines *mts.* Italy **22 D6** 44.00N 11.00E
Appalachian Mts. U.S.A. **53 K6** 39.30N 78.00W
Arabian Sea Asia **30 F2** 19.00N 65.00E
Arafura Sea Austa. **64 D5** 9.00S 135.00E
Araguaína Brazil **58 G6** 7.16S 48.18W
Araguari Brazil **58 G4** 18.38S 48.13W
Aral Sea Asia **30 E5** 45.00N 60.00E
Archangel Russian Fed. **21 H5** 64.32N 41.10E
Arctic Ocean 68
Arequipa Peru **58 B4** 16.25S 71.32W
Argentina S. America **57 E3** 35.00S 65.00W
Arica Chile **56 D5** 18.30S 70.20W
Arkansas *r.* U.S.A. **53 J6** 33.50N 91.00W
Armenia Asia **30 D5** 40.00N 45.00E
Arnhem Land *f.* Australia **64 D4** 13.00S 132.30E
Aruba *i.* Lesser Antilles **56 D8** 12.30N 70.00W
Arusha Tanzania **42 G4** 3.21S 36.40E
Ashford England **11 G2** 51.08N 0.53E
Asia 28-29
Asmara Eritrea **42 G6** 15.20N 38.58E
Asunción Paraguay **58 E2** 25.15S 57.40W
Atacama Desert S. America **57 D4** 20.00S 69.00W
Athens Greece **20 F2** 37.59N 23.42E
Atlanta U.S.A. **53 K5** 33.45N 84.23W
Atlantic Ocean **70 G7**
Atlas Mts. Africa **42 C8** 33.00N 4.00W
Auckland New Zealand **65 H2** 36.52S 174.45E
Australia Austa. **64** 25.00S 135.00E
Austria Europe **20 E3** 47.30N 14.00E
Ayers Rock *see* Uluru Australia **64**
Ayr Scotland **10 D4** 55.28N 4.37W
Azerbaijan Asia **30 D5** 40.10N 47.50E
Azov, Sea of Ukraine **21 G3** 46.00N 36.30E

B

Baffin B. Canada **52 M10** 74.00N 70.00W
Baffin I. Canada **52 L9** 68.50N 70.00W
Baghdad Iraq **30 D4** 33.20N 44.26E
Bahrain Asia **30 E3** 26.00N 50.35E
Baikal, L. Russian Fed. **32 C9** 53.30N 108.00E
Baja California *pen.* Mexico **53 H5** 27.00N 113.00W

Baku Azerbaijan **30 D5** 40.22N 49.53E
Balbina, Represa de *resr.* Brazil **58 E7** 1.30S 60.00W
Balearic Is. Spain **20 D2** 39.30N 2.30E
Balkan Mts. Bulgaria **20 F3** 42.50N 24.30E
Balkhash, L. Kazakhstan **28 F6** 46.51N 75.00E
Baltic Sea Europe **20 E4** 56.30N 19.00E
Baltimore U.S.A. **52 L6** 39.18N 76.38W
Bamako Mali **42 C6** 12.40N 7.59W
Bandar Seri Begawan Brunei **33 D4** 4.56N 114.58E
Bangalore India **31 G2** 12.58N 77.35E
Bangkok Thailand **33 C5** 13.45N 100.35E
Bangladesh Asia **31 H3** 24.00N 90.00E
Bangui C.A.R. **42 E5** 4.23N 18.37E
Baotou China **32 D8** 40.38N 109.59E
Barbados Lesser Antilles **56 F8** 13.20N 59.40W
Barcelona Spain **20 D3** 41.25N 2.10E
Barents Sea Arctic Oc. **28 D7** 73.00N 40.00E
Barquisimeto Venezuela **56 E8** 10.03N 69.18W
Barranquilla Colombia **56 D8** 11.00N 74.50W
Basel Switz. **20 D3** 47.33N 7.36E
Bass Str. Australia **64 E2** 39.45S 146.00E
Bath England **11 E2** 51.22N 2.22W
Beijing China **32 D7** 39.55N 116.25E
Beirut Lebanon **30 C4** 33.52N 35.30E
Belarus Europe **20 F4** 53.00N 28.00E
Belém Brazil **58 G7** 1.27S 48.29W
Belfast N. Ireland **11 D4** 54.36N 5.57W
Belgium Europe **20 D4** 51.00N 4.30E
Belgrade Serb. **20 F3** 44.49N 20.28E
Belize C. America **53 K4** 17.00N 88.30W
Belmopan Belize **53 K4** 17.25N 88.46W
Belo Horizonte Brazil **59 H4** 19.45S 43.53W
Ben Nevis *mtn.* Scotland **10 D5** 56.48N 5.00W
Bengal, B. of Indian Oc. **31 H2** 17.00N 89.00E
Benin Africa **42 D5** 9.00N 2.30E
Benin, Bight of *b.* Africa **42 D5** 5.30N 3.00E
Bergen Norway **20 D5** 60.23N 5.20E
Bering Sea N. America/Asia **29 N6** 60.00N 170.00E
Berlin Germany **20 E4** 52.32N 13.25E
Bermuda *i.* Atlantic Oc. **53 M6** 32.18N 65.00W
Bern Switz. **20 D3** 46.57N 7.26E
Berwick-upon-Tweed England **10 E4** 55.46N 2.00W
Bhutan Asia **31 I3** 27.25N 90.00E
Bié Plateau *f.* Angola **43 E3** 13.00S 16.00E
Birmingham England **11 F3** 52.30N 1.55W
Biscay, B. of France **20 C3** 45.30N 3.00W
Bissau Guinea-Bissau **42 B6** 11.52N 15.39W

Black Sea Europe **21 G3** 43.00N 35.00E
Blackburn England **11 E3** 53.44N 2.30W
Blackpool England **11 E3** 53.48N 3.03W
Blanc, Mont *mtn.* Europe **20 D3** 45.50N 6.52E
Bogotá Colombia **56 D7** 4.38N 74.05W
Bolivia S. America **58 C4** 17.00S 65.00W
Bologna Italy **22 D6** 44.30N 11.20E
Bolton England **11 E3** 53.35N 2.26W
Bombay *see* Mumbai India **29**
Bonn Germany **20 D4** 50.44N 7.06E
Bordeaux France **20 C3** 44.50N 0.34W
Borneo *i.* Asia **33 D4** 1.00N 114.00E
Bosnia-Herzegovina Europe **20 E3** 44.00N 18.00E
Boston U.S.A. **52 L7** 42.15N 71.05W
Bothnia, G. of Europe **20 E5** 63.30N 20.30E
Botswana Africa **43 F2** 22.00S 24.00E
Bournemouth England **11 F2** 50.43N 1.53W
Bradford England **11 F3** 53.47N 1.45W
Brasília Brazil **58 G4** 15.54S 47.50W
Bratislava Slovakia **20 E3** 48.10N 17.10E
Brazil S. America **58-59** 10.00S 52.00W
Brazilian Highlands Brazil **58 G5** 17.00S 48.00W
Brazzaville Congo **42 E4** 4.14S 15.14E
Brighton England **11 F2** 50.50N 0.09W
Brisbane Australia **64 F3** 27.30S 153.00E
Bristol England **11 E2** 51.26N 2.35W
Bristol Channel England/Wales **11 D2** 51.17N 3.20W
British Isles Europe **18 D5** 54.00N 5.00W
Brunei Asia **33 D4** 4.56N 114.58E
Brussels Belgium **20 D4** 50.50N 4.23E
Bucharest Romania **20 F3** 44.25N 26.06E
Budapest Hungary **20 E3** 47.30N 19.03E
Buenos Aires Argentina **57 F3** 34.40S 58.30W
Bujumbura Burundi **42 F4** 3.22S 29.21E
Bulgaria Europe **20 F3** 42.30N 25.00E
Burkina Africa **42 C6** 12.15N 1.30W
Burma *see* Myanmar Asia **29**
Bursa Turkey **20 F3** 40.11N 29.04E
Burundi Africa **42 G4** 3.30S 30.00E

C

Caernarfon Wales **11 D3** 53.08N 4.17W
Cagliari Italy **22 C3** 39.14N 9.07E
Cairns Australia **64 E4** 16.51S 145.43E
Cairo Egypt **42 G8** 30.03N 31.15E
Calais France **20 D4** 50.57N 1.50E
Calcutta *see* Kolkata India **31**